teach yourself

stand-up comedy

stand-up comedy
logan murray

Launched in 1938, the **teach yourself** series grew rapidly in response to the world's wartime needs. Loved and trusted by over 50 million readers, the series has continued to respond to society's changing interests and passions and now, 70 years on, includes over 500 titles, from Arabic and Beekeeping to Yoga and Zulu. What would you like to learn?

be where you want to be with **teach yourself**

For UK order enquiries: please contact Bookpoint Ltd, 130 Milton Park, Abingdon, Oxon, OX14 4SB. Telephone: +44 (0) 1235 827720. Fax: +44 (0) 1235 400454. Lines are open 09.00–17.00, Monday to Saturday, with a 24-hour message answering service. Details about our titles and how to order are available at www.teachyourself.co.uk

For USA order enquiries: please contact McGraw-Hill Customer Services, PO Box 545, Blacklick, OH 43004-0545, USA. Telephone: 1-800-722-4726. Fax: 1-614-755-5645.

For Canada order enquiries: please contact McGraw-Hill Ryerson Ltd, 300 Water St, Whitby, Ontario, L1N 9B6, Canada. Telephone: 905 430 5000. Fax: 905 430 5020.

Long renowned as the authoritative source for self-guided learning – with more than 50 million copies sold worldwide – the **teach yourself** series includes over 500 titles in the fields of languages, crafts, hobbies, business, computing and education.

British Library Cataloguing in Publication Data: a catalogue record for this title is available from the British Library.

Library of Congress Catalog Card Number: on file.

First published in UK 2008 by Hodder Education, part of Hachette Livre UK, 338 Euston Road, London, NW1 3BH.

First published in US 2007 by The McGraw-Hill Companies, Inc.

This edition published 2007.

The **teach yourself** name is a registered trade mark of Hodder Headline.

Copyright © 2007 Logan Murray

Typeset by Transet Limited, Coventry, England.
Printed in Great Britain for Hodder Education, an Hachette Livre UK Company, 338 Euston Road, London NW1 3BH, by CPI Cox & Wyman, Reading, Berkshire RG1 8EX.

The publisher has used its best endeavours to ensure that the URLs for external websites referred to in this book are correct and active at the time of going to press. However, the publisher and the author have no responsibility for the websites and can make no guarantee that a site will remain live or that the content will remain relevant, decent or appropriate.

Hachette Livre UK's policy is to use papers that are natural, renewable and recyclable products and made from wood grown in sustainable forests. The logging and manufacturing processes are expected to conform to the environmental regulations of the country of origin.

Impression number   10 9 8 7 6 5 4 3 2
Year   2010 2009 2008

contents

acknowledgements

Thanks to all the comedians who contributed to this book.

Thanks also to all the comics at the Fortnight Club who have made the past decade such a pleasure to host. And to Maddi Carberi for keeping the club going despite numerous venue changes – a thankless task! You are much missed on our Monday evenings.

Thanks for the Comedy Course 700, who've taught me so much and made me laugh far too much. And a special thanks to Hils Jago for her tireless work in organising everything.

I'm also grateful to Steve Armstrong for inadvertently setting this whole thing in train, also to Victoria Roddam for her invaluable suggestions.

Lastly, a massive thanks to Katy Bagshaw for teaching me the meaning of punctuation.

about the author

Logan Murray has been a working comedian since 1984.

Over the years, he has performed in every conceivable venue, from a converted public lavatory to 3,000 people at the Glastonbury Festival, in the UK and throughout the world.

During his career he has written for TV and radio. He has appeared in variety shows, sitcoms, documentaries, panel shows and game shows.

In 1994 Logan Murray created his alter ego, the monstrously bitter, tired old showbiz hack Ronnie Rigsby who has an impressive résumé of live dates and TV and radio appearances to rival his own!

Logan Murray was also one half of the infamous 90s double act 'Bib and Bob' with Jerry Sadowitz. They have appeared all over the country, including a West End run at the Criterion Theatre (the police were called twice and the critics lauded it as the best bad taste show ever).

He has directed the stage shows of award-winning comedians, lectured at Middlesex University and teaches comedy at the BBC.

Logan Murray regularly holds highly acclaimed courses in London and is acknowledged as one of the best comedy tutors in the UK.

introduction

1985

I have just smuggled myself out of hospital, where I have been bed bound, in excruciating agony from rheumatic fever. I am shaking and sweating, leaning on a stick, feeling that I have just made the most stupid mistake of my young life.

My destination is the London Comedy Store, where I have been booked to perform five minutes for a BBC Radio Show called *Cabaret Upstairs*. I have cancelled every gig in my diary, one by one, from the hospital ward's public telephone, as I get progressively sicker – but I'm determined not to give up my first radio job.

The compère announces my name and I limp on to the stage, trying to fake a normal healthy stride. I deliver my first line and the well-primed audience roll over, like a big puppy dog, with laughter. For the next five minutes I feel brilliant.

1995

I'm on stage for the second time that evening, having raced across London to 'double up' at another gig. If anything, this audience seems even better than the first one. Probably because it's later in the evening and they are more warmed up after an interval...

I'm half way through a joke when I have a strange feeling of déjà vu. There is an awful sinking feeling that I'm repeating a joke that I've just told this crowd.

Intellectually, I know that I'm probably remembering the earlier gig, but my gut tells me that I'll get to the punch line and the audience will give me a look of pity. This feeling is so strong that instead of nailing the gag, I say it as – if – I – am – wading – through – treacle. I avoid the looks of pity, but now the audience are looking at me as if I'm slightly constipated, I resolve to pick up the pace!

2005

I'm standing at the back of a smoky, packed Comedy Club in North London. The audience is excited and boisterous. They are waiting to see seven brand new comics taking their first fledgling steps into the gloriously tawdry world of showbiz. What the audience doesn't know is two have pulled out at the last minute through sheer fear. I am frantically scribbling down a new running order and trying to dragoon two more comics, who just came down to watch, into filling the stage time. I'm standing quite close to the gents' toilet. If I listen very carefully, I can hear the first act being sick... Ah, the glamour!

I've been making a living as a stand-up comic for over 20 years. To be honest, this is the only job I've ever known.

The hours are great, 20 minutes a night, three or four evenings a week. The pay is fantastic. I'm my own boss. I never have to set the alarm to avoid the early morning rush hour. I genuinely look forward to going to work and cannot imagine ever wanting to retire. This business has allowed me to perform all over the world, as far west as Colorado and as far east as the Gulf States. It has lead to some really interesting (and, occasionally, strange) jobs in TV and Radio. I've presented TV game shows too cheesy for words; had tiny parts in several very good sitcoms; supplied the voices for some well known cartoon characters and, for some bizarre reason, played a computer generated fish *twice* for two separate terrestrial television projects. I've written for Radio, TV, the stage and, occasionally, for magazines. I mention all these things not to brag, but just to point out that none of these experiences would have come my way had I not been a comedian.

To me, stand-up is its own reward. It's not something you do to become famous (although, it would be nice) or rich (although, again, I wouldn't complain).

We do this job because on some basic level we need to stand up in front of a bunch of strangers and make them laugh.

Give me 70 or 80 people in a room above a pub, and I'm never happier.

I've done big gigs, little gigs, great gigs and scary gigs that have taken years off my life. I've been drowned out by bands at the Reading Festival, had a performing epiphany at the Glastonbury Festival and lost thousands of pounds at the Edinburgh Fringe.

What compels a certain type of person to choose this life as a career?

What fuels this desire that comedians have for getting up on stage?

Is it a cry for attention? Arrested development? Not enough love as a child?

Perhaps the answer is much simpler. Most comedians, if they are honest, will tell you that nothing can beat the feeling of making other human beings laugh. That is, I suspect, the real reason why comics spend far too many nights, red-eyed and hunched over the steering wheel, heading for home, fuelled by motorway coffee and chocolate, having entertained a room full of people in some far flung corner of Britain. The best party in the world would compare poorly to that time in front of the microphone. The finest wines are tame in comparison to the adrenaline rush experienced on stage – plus, you don't have to worry about a hangover the next morning.

On a good night, just as they step up for an encore, a comedian could believe that they have the easiest job in the world.

Sometimes the show seems to be over all too soon. The nature of performing is that it is entirely ephemeral: unlike a painter or sculptor, there is no physical artefact left behind, that we can point to and say, 'Look, that's me being funny.'

We are only as good as our last gig.

If we keep our wits about us, we can learn from the bad shows and always admit room for improvement after the great gigs. It's all part of the learning process, and in comedy there's always something new to learn.

So you want to be a stand-up comedian?

Everyone has the ability to be funny.

Over the past five years I've had the great pleasure of teaching over 700 people how to perform stand-up comedy. Almost all of them took part in a final show open to the public. Out of those 700, most had a blast at their very first gig. More importantly, so did the audience. So much so that these new comics got bitten by the bug and (rather like me) became seduced into this lifestyle. A fair number, a year later, liked the lifestyle so much – and were having enough success – that they became professional comedians. You've probably seen one or two of them.

I wish I could say that this high success rate is purely down to me being the best teacher in the world, but I think it's truer to say that the ability to be funny is a natural human trait. We all have the ability to make others laugh, to set strangers at their ease, to play with ideas (often, the essence of a joke), and to communicate those ideas to others. If you think about it, there is a great deal of evolutionary sense in breeding these traits into individuals. If you could use humour to defuse a situation, or to bond with the rest of your group, you would probably increase your chances for survival. These people would probably live long enough to breed. The miserable, uncooperative types, lacking imagination, would probably die alone and unloved.

Serves them right. No one loves a whinger.

Chances are the people who could deal with the strangers over the hill and perhaps got along with them long enough to trade with them, stood a better chance of passing their sociable genes onto the next generation.

Obviously, a closer study of human history might show that we are very good at killing each other too, but that subject is covered in my companion volume to this book, provisionally titled *Teach Yourself Mass Murder*.

What makes people funny?

We all find funny people sexier. It's an attractive trait in our prospective partners. Why does the phrase 'good sense of humour' litter Lonely Hearts columns? Isn't it true to say that, no matter how shy we are, we all like to think of ourselves as possessing a keen sense of humour? That's probably true for you, isn't it? Even if you've never admitted it to anyone else.

Have you ever had that experience at a party where, perhaps fuelled by a glass of wine to loosen your inhibitions, perhaps standing with a number of close friends and newly met acquaintances, you've all started to make each other laugh – *without even trying?* No one is resorting to 'jokes', no one is trying to 'take control'; you are all just chipping in, each adding to the previous person's comments, generally being really playful and having a laugh. A feeling of well being washes over you and everyone else. You are having an enormous amount of fun. You feel better than you have done for days. Of course, you recognize this experience, because it's what human beings do. It's also why people go to comedy clubs, to experience this sense of giddy joy. To have a laugh.

In essence, a comedian is trying to recreate that sense of joy, or 'a bloody good party', while they are on stage. There is no difference entertaining six people in the kitchen at a party or 60 in a small comedy club or 6,000 in the Comedy Tent at the Glastonbury Festival. It's just a matter of degree.

So, let's entertain the idea that people can be naturally funny.

What makes a stand-up different from other performers?

Stand-up is a very naked medium: it's just you and the audience

A comic hasn't got the luxury of blaming the script or the director or a fellow actor for giving him or her the wrong cue. They are alone in front of the paying crowd. Unlike other performing arts, I can't excuse a prolonged silence from my audience with the notion that 'I'm really making them *think*, tonight.' If I don't hear the audience laughing with certain regularity, then I know I haven't done my job.

The fact that there are no barriers between you and the audience makes it a very pure art form. Your relationship is solely with the audience. You are not reciting some lines; you are telling them a story, here and now. You are the author, the director and the actor. If they don't like you, there is no one else to blame. But if they love you, then the credit is all yours!

There is an immediacy to stand-up

If you make an audience laugh, you know you are doing your job. If you make them laugh enough, the people who run clubs have to book you. You begin to build up a reputation.

The life of a comedian is very empowering

You pick up the phone, *you* get the gigs, *you* make people laugh. Word gets around, other people want to book you, so *you* pick up the phone again, *you* ring the new numbers people have given you, *you* get the gigs... and so it goes. There is no boss telling you to work harder or that you're failing to meet this month's targets; there is no casting agent suggesting that you are too tall or too short, too old or too fat for the part. It is very difficult to believe critics who tell you that you are not very good, if the whole room is laughing.

The secret of stand-up comedy

The most important thing to remember in a stand-up career is *persevere.*

If you keep performing, you *will* get better.

If you keep performing, you *will* come up with new ideas.

If you keep at it, people *will* offer you strange, often lucrative, jobs that you could never have imagined.

You could be the funniest person in the world, but if you never try your ideas out in front of the world, the world will never know.

How to use this book

Treat this book as a big bag of tricks.

All the exercises have been tried and tested by countless people in the past but that doesn't mean that you have to like them all. Some comedians gravitate towards the word play games; some prefer the showing off games. It would be a good idea to try all the exercises at least once, if you can – I can appreciate that some of the group activities may prove difficult if there's just you or only two or three of you trying out ideas in a workshop style session. You may find it useful to return to the exercises at least one more time (perhaps after you've started performing), just to see how differently you react to them when you have had some performance experience.

As a general point, feel free to return to themes and ideas again and again as you write and perform. You should never feel, 'Oh well, I covered this subject.' As we will find out later on, you can always find a new twist to an old subject. Remember Heraclitus' old adage: 'A man cannot enter the same river twice, for he is not the same man, nor is it the same river.' Everything, including ourselves, always changes. The way you write about relationships would not be the same at the beginning of a love affair as it would be if you put pen to paper just after you had been dumped. It would be a lazy comedian indeed who decided that they have exhausted a subject forever.

Write for your own pleasure

While we are on the subject of writing, I would strongly suggest that you get in the habit of writing for *yourself*. That is to say, write (and perform) what *you* think is funny, rather than trying to guess what your hypothetical audience wants you to say. All worthwhile comedians talk about what matters to them. That's what the audience want to hear – *your* opinion on things. Have confidence that what you have to say on a subject is worth hearing. Your perspective is unique, the audience are desperate to hear your point of view. They know what *they* think, so tell them something new.

Have fun doing the work in this book. If it starts to seem like hard work, take a break. All creativity comes out of play, so don't treat the time improving your comedy as a prison sentence.

Use the exercises in this book as starting points to create your own games. If you can find an interesting 'twist' to the instructions, feel free to give it a go. There are no rules where creativity is concerned, except to say that if an exercise feels like fun when you are doing it and leaves you with a giddy desire to show off what you have just created, then you've probably done the right thing, *even if it contradicts the rules for the particular exercise*. You're the boss.

Working individually

The vast majority of the preparation work that a comedian does is solitary. That involves a degree of discipline on your part, especially when you're staring at a blank piece of paper desperately trying to remember if there is anything remotely funny in your head.

Set guidelines for your work.

Top tip

Always carry a pen and a little notebook with you because you never can tell when inspiration will hit you. If you can bear to look a bit weird, carry one of those pocket voice recorders with you and mutter the funny idea into it before it evaporates. But think twice before doing it on a first date!

On top of this, tell yourself that you are going to set aside an hour (at least) every day to write. That is time over and above when you may be jotting down an idea that occurs on the bus.

Most importantly – and certainly when you begin – allow yourself the freedom of *not* being funny. Allow yourself to explore ideas without insisting that there is a punch line at the end of every sentence. This period of time is set aside for you to play – something which many of us were actively discouraged to do after childhood – so it may take time to relearn how to have fun again.

Set yourself a task

For example, you could:

- write a list of all the kids who bullied you at school, and imagine where they are today (if there was any justice in the world!);
- write down crossword puzzle clues written by a hopeless alcoholic or someone who's just got divorced;
- draw a four-panel cartoon showing the rest of your life;
- write a list of your top ten favourite films of all time and why;
- write a love poem written by a sanitary engineer or a traffic warden;

- write up a list of things **never** to say to a new partner;
- describe the worst Olympic sport (real or made up) and explain why;
- list obvious clichés in horror films;
- list some really bad ideas for Christmas presents for your family, and why;
- write a synopsis of *War and Peace* in under 50 words;
- describe the plot of *Macbeth* in 20 words, then see if you can cut it down to 10;
- recount your worst fashion mistake ever;
- list your favourite words, explaining why.

You will find some more interesting ideas and tasks to inspire you in later chapters: Chapter 05 lists quite a few creativity exercises; Chapter 07 will take you through several workshops designed to help you uncover funny material. There is also an appendix detailing lots of group comedy games for you to use if you are lucky enough to be working with a group of like-minded people.

Writer's block

Setting yourself little writing games is possibly one of the best ways for a budding comedian to avoid writer's block. It breaks things down into bite-sized chunks and makes every piece of writing a game to play, rather than a task to complete.

The more you write, the more you are exercising those creative muscles, so keep to your daily or weekly schedule. And don't judge yourself too harshly!

You may find, once you start, that the creative floodgates open and all this stuff locked up in your brain starts pouring out. Unfortunately for your social life, inspiration rarely follows a nine-to-five schedule. Friends and loved ones don't always understand that you have to strike while the inspiration is hot; often, if they're not performers themselves, they won't understand that you have to write it down *then and there* even if it means turning on the bedside lamp at two in the morning. So a little bit of sensitivity may be called for on your part. Usually, once they are made aware that comedy is your career, most partners will forgive the occasional burning of the midnight oil.

The two key qualities that an aspiring comic working alone should cultivate are discipline and perseverance: discipline to get the work done and perseverance to keep battering at the comedy industry until they begin to notice you. It can seem a very hard road when you've just been booed off the stage, but take heart that every comedian worth their salt has been booed off at some time in their career. By learning from their mistakes and by not giving up, they have become better performers.

Working in groups

This method has a lot to recommend it. Three or four like-minded new comedians brainstorming ideas will probably cover more ground through simple synergy alone than a solo comic would. Think about the way most American sitcoms are written: a bullpen of 10 or 20 writers will sit round a table and throw ideas at each other. This can, with the right people, be a very productive way of working. Ownership issues of who wrote what joke don't have to rear their ugly heads if clear guidelines are set at the beginning. At its root, you know if an idea is really yours or someone else's.

Here are some simple working ground rules:

- No ideas are to be shot down in flames whilst they are still in development.
- No one person is in charge.
- Try to say, metaphorically at least, 'yes, and...' to an idea rather than 'no'. Saying yes builds on an idea. Saying no is effectively closing off a discussion. 'What if...' is a much better premise for a comedian to work with than 'It could never happen.'
- Whilst general ideas are up for grabs (for instance 'relationships' is such a general subject heading, as to be almost meaningless), specific ideas based on your attitude or experience belong to *you*. For example, I have some jokes about a diabetic cat I once looked after. If I had presented these to a group of other comics, and then found the next week they had all come up with their own diabetic cat material, I'd be a little suspicious.

Those three or four people can also act as a support group for each other, pooling information about venues and being a friendly face in a crowd. Also, the presence of other people will galvanize the individual comic into working, rather than deciding to do some 'research' watching the TV, or staring out of the window.

Working in a group forces you to think how you can best present your ideas to other people. It stops it becoming just a mental exercise and makes you have to perform – stand-up is, after all, a social activity.

A few of the games and exercises in this book (and all the ones listed in the appendix) have been devised to work with a partner or in a group. The logic behind this is that it lets the individual comedian off the hook, by letting them react (hopefully in a funny way) to what their partner is doing. It also forces the comedian to up their game before trying it out in front of an audience. Chances are, if a funny idea can be communicated to one other person, it can probably be made to work in front of a paying crowd.

Comedy workshops

There are a number of professionally lead comedy courses running throughout the world. It provides an opportunity for the new comic to 'road test' or 'workshop' their ideas in a safe, supportive environment. Many famous comedians of the past 20 years have taken part in them. If you live in a major city with a handful (or more) of comedy clubs, then there is a strong likelihood that there is a course running somewhere near you.

A few common sense questions should indicate whether it's a good course. Has it got a good reputation? Are other comedians recommending it? Is it run by a comedian? What is the standard of the comedians who have done the course? All these things can be checked out before the aspiring comic is persuaded to part with their hard earned cash. A good course can, week by week, give the aspiring stand-up some concrete goals to work towards: setting homework, refining material or looking at an individual's presentation skills. Just as a car mechanic needs a workshop to tinker with a vehicle, a new comedian may need a workshop situation to fine-tune their routine.

A workshop is a forum to experiment and to take greater risks than you might do by yourself. You could, perhaps, discover a unique performance style that no amount of working alone, or even in small groups around a kitchen table, could uncover. It also provides an opportunity for you to hone your craft in front of a large group of sympathetic strangers who are also trying to do the same thing. A good course should increase your chances of hitting the ground running when you get out there in front of paying audiences, as you've committed most of your 'rookie' mistakes in the workshops. You will also be used to performing in front of people.

Collectively, 15 or 20 people are cleverer than one individual, and the group can goad the individual to greater efforts. Fifteen or 20 people also offer a greater opportunity to network.

The only possible downside to a workshop might be that it's led by someone trying to impose his or her ideas of comedy on you. I would be very suspicious of a didactic teacher who said that there was only one way of doing things – their way!

Before you go any further...

- Buy a notebook.
- Draw up a schedule.
- Choose one of the ideas mentioned earlier under the section of 'Working individually' and do it.

part one

theory

01

where do jokes come from?

In this chapter you will learn:
- the mechanisms that lie underneath a joke
- how to kick-start your own comic creativity
- why your personal opinions matter most when you are writing jokes.

'I rather like those books where each chapter begins with a quotation.'

Ramsey Dukes

What is laughter? It seems to be a very pleasurable activity that we all share, yet find very hard to analyse. It is a phenomenon not completely under our control: laughter can strike when we least desire it (giggling in church); it is hard to fake a laugh (ask an actor), but it is possible – sometimes – to suppress it. Every attempt to describe this state falls short of the truth. Calling it a 'semi-involuntary reflex triggered by diverse stimuli', as many behavioural psychologists have, seems to be missing the point and will probably not get us invited to too many parties.

It's a mystery. Trying to explain laughter is a bit like trying to describe time: we all experience it, but it is very hard to put into words. Perhaps it has something to do with a loss of control in safe conditions. Think of the expressions we use to describe the phenomenon: 'I was on the floor'; 'I nearly wet myself'; 'I was crying with laughter' or 'I fell out of my seat'. They all suggest a sanctioned loss of control.

Laughter acts like a balm to the body and the spirit. We feel all bright eyed and bushy tailed after a good laugh; our body pumps out endorphins and we feel more human. But we are really none the wiser in understanding the strange alchemy that goes on in our brain when someone makes us laugh. Luckily, no one expects comedians to know *why* we laugh; the public are only concerned whether we know *how* to make people laugh.

Perhaps we are on safer ground if we ask where the roots of comedy lie. But to address this, we need to broaden our remit and ask ourselves what fuels the act of creation.

Do we create funny ideas or do they come and find us?

Obviously, the comedian is responsible for everything that comes out of their mouth – they are the creator. But are they the *conscious* creator? It seems to me that most of the jokes that I make already exist 'out there' in some strange realm of ideas, and that the comedian travels towards them. Sometimes there is an awful lot of hard work involved in getting to that place, but that final leap of faith – that inspiration – seems to arrive from outside yourself. Creativity comes from beyond our everyday conscious selves. Indeed, our everyday selves can often get in the way of being creative.

We are trained from an early age never to trust the first draft of anything. Instead of learning the 'fun' of language, we are taught to conjugate verbs and parse sentences. When painting we are expected to redraft the piece two or three times to make it technically better; we learn not to write how we speak, but to adopt a strange artificial 'grown up' way of writing, full of bombastic phrases which no real adults use outside of a news report or a House of Commons debate. It all becomes a bit dry and dusty.

We are encouraged to learn by rote and disengage our creativity. If we *are* asked to be creative, we are encouraged to think that the process is hard, and to forget how much fun it was to play with ideas when we were younger.

The pity of it is that creativity and craft don't have to be divorced from each other.

Most of us need to reconnect with our sense of play. We have to kill that little demon living on our shoulders telling us that what we're doing isn't good enough.

Practical creative games

Here are a few games that may help you start to rediscover your sense of playfulness. You'll need at least one other person for some of them – certainly for the last one. The reasoning behind this is that the presence of another person will make you both try harder; also it gives you someone to react to. In all of these games, try to let yourself off the hook (they are supposed to be fun, after all) and don't take charge! If you make your partner the boss and they make you the boss, then you won't let your conscious self try to take control and mess it up.

Having said that, most of the group games could be tweaked into a solitary exercise, with a bit of thought, and it's worth reading through them anyway as they may give you helpful ideas.

TV commentary

(This could be done alone or with other people)

Turn down the television and supply the voices for the show. My personal favourites are old films and daytime makeover shows. Some people prefer soap opera or even adverts. Let your commentaries be opinionated.

Problem pages

(This could be done as a solitary exercise)

Read aloud to your partner(s) the letters on a problem page. Try to add the occasional sentence or word that might exaggerate or alter the problem, perhaps taking it into a completely different area. Read out the answer and feel free to alter that too. Practise being flippant and learn to say the wrong thing at the wrong time. Be callous.

Letters written into local newspapers are also quite good sources for subversion.

Also, feel free to remember tried and tested group activities like Charades. Anything that gets you out of your head and up onto your feet, showing how creative you actually are, is probably a good thing.

Timeless classics

(A solo writing game)

Write the first paragraph of a famous book that you **haven't** read and only have the barest passing knowledge of. But write it as if the author was obsessed with something incredibly minor, like teeth or shoes or door handles. How will that affect the text? For instance, what would *War and Peace* be like if Tolstoy had been scared of heights?

A liar's biography

(A solo writing game)

Write a biography about your glorious life and brilliant career as if you have a very weak grip on reality. For example, you may be delusional or borderline psychotic, self serving or just a very bitter person. Be as detailed or as broad as you like.

One word story

Two or more of you tell a story out loud, but you are each only allowed to give one word of the sentence. So if there were three people involved (A, B and C), it might look a little like this:

A: I

B: woke

C: up

A: today

B: to

C: find

A: a

B: frog

C: on

A: my

B: pillow.

Make sure the story makes sense and that there are no jarring bits, such as one of you starting a new sentence before the old one is finished. Turn your brain off, listen to the other person (or people) and have fun. Eventually, try to get up to conversational speed, but start off slowly.

Some modern theories of humour

Many people over the years have tried to come up with a universal theory of why we find things funny. Many of them are fascinating, but fail at being truly universal: at best they describe one type of humour.

With hindsight, we can recognize that these theories are embedded in their time; unduly influenced by the prejudices and concerns of their world. All writers fall prey to this, up to and including Aristotle, who committed to paper the questionable idea that 'Women haven't got souls'. (Do you think he wrote that after a particularly bitter break up?) This unquestioning cultural bias permeates everything, but is often only visible after the event – like costume drama films of the 1960s that give the heroine a beehive, or the hero a quiff. Only when viewed later do they stick out like a sore thumb. This is true with theories in comedy, which are as prone to fashion as anything else. So, having primed ourselves to be aware of cultural bias, let's take a closer look.

Humour as a weapon

Charles Darwin popularized the general view that most aspects of civilized behaviour were nothing more than complicated versions of territorial behaviour common to most animals. Emotions, he suggested, were dangerous primal forces that had to be controlled by our self-made rituals. Beneath this polite, social facade lurked more ancient impulses.

Rather than physically attack someone (and possibly lose the fight), humour allowed the protagonist to symbolically kill his or her victim; or, if you prefer, to 'put them down'. When a comedian uses a heckle put down to shut up a noisy member of the audience, they are not so much trying to win a battle of wits as to re-establish the animal hierarchy. Like any would-be alpha male or female they are saying: 'I'm in charge, listen to me!'

Humour, Darwin says, is all about dominance and control. The victims of our jokes are suffering the suppressed fury of our killer instinct.

Is his theory universal? It certainly chimes with the man who popularized the idea of 'nature red in tooth and claw', but it doesn't explain how, if all jokes are predatory, we can find ourselves laughing at the absurd, or ourselves.

Where is the killer instinct in the following jokes?

'What's brown and sticky? A stick.' (An ancient kid's joke)

'I bought a box of instant water, but didn't know what to add...' (Steve Wright)

'I'm really worried about the state of the world, ladies and gentlemen. I mean if things carry on the way they are... they'll stay the same.' (Pat Condell)

Humour as a way of mocking others

French philosopher Henri Bergson wrote an essay called 'Laughter' detailing what he thought was the origin and impetus of humour. In it he states that what we find funny is '...the mechanical attributes of inertia, rigidity and repetitiveness as they impinge on human affairs.' In other words, we laugh when we find other people reduced to unthinking responses, or who are on 'automatic pilot', or whose behaviour puts them on a collision course with the world. We laugh because we see others becoming inflexible.

This could mean something as simple as watching someone walk into a lamppost (slapstick), but it could mean we laugh when people's brains fall out of gear: we laugh at someone who can't stop mentioning diets in front of a fat person and digs a deeper and deeper hole for themselves. There is a scene in an Austin Powers film (and also in an earlier John Hughes movie, *Uncle Buck*) where the hero notices a mole on someone's face and, despite his best efforts, can't stop fixating on it. Another example would be when Basil Fawlty tells his staff, 'Don't mention the war' to some German guests staying in his hotel, and then, when he is with them, is able to do little else. These comedians are portraying people trapped by their own mental programming and nothing their conscious mind can do will lift them out of it. That is their tragedy but, luckily for us, our comedy.

Similarly, when people are responding automatically, without taking changing circumstances into consideration, we can find ourselves laughing at them and their inappropriate reaction to a situation; like the befuddled politician who finds himself at election time kissing the hands of voters and vigorously shaking their babies, rather than the other way round.

Humour as a means of revealing a taboo

Sigmund Freud's book of 1905, *Jokes and their Relation to the Unconscious*, takes the broad view that laughter is caused by repressed material which has not previously been allowed an airing. Freud says that often we will laugh at the shock of hearing things that haven't previously been said; or more importantly, things which shouldn't have been said. A joke uncovers that which is taboo. Rather like the child pointing out, in the *Emperor's New Clothes* that the monarch is naked, the comedian reveals what is under the surface, and says that which usually remains unsaid.

One of Freud's interests lay in finding out why a shared joke was pleasurable and why someone would want to tell them, or pass on old jokes to a new audience. What satisfaction is derived from this situation?

Apart from wanting to share the 'eureka' moment of the punchline, an obvious pleasure lies in sharing some dirty little secret, especially if the joke revolves around a shared prejudice, for example: all mother in laws are monsters; all Scottish people are tight with money or all Essex women are stupid.

This opens up an interesting dilemma for the comedian, of which more will be said later: do we give the audience what we think they want us to hear? In other words, do we pander to their views? Or do we tell them what we want to say? Do we confirm their world view (and possibly their prejudices) or do we challenge them? How much of the individual comic is a crowd pleaser and how much is he or she an artist?

Humour as play

Arthur Koestler, in *The Act of Creation*, suggests that the value of humour may lie in its ability to allow people to think along two different lines of thought at once. Joking becomes a game, an opportunity to exercise those mental muscles allowing us to practise rehearsing possible future situations; even if the joke seems not to relate to the world, by juxtaposing two dissimilar subjects that don't usually go together, the comic is playing with possibilities.

Humour's function, according to Koestler, is that it forces people to do what they do best: it forces them to think.

Any art we create (says Koestler) will cause the audience to make new connections or see something in a new way. It is the 'spark' our brains generate in bringing these dissimilar objects together that creates the moment when we go 'Aha!' If we're looking at the roof of the Sistine Chapel, it might cause a sharp intake of breath. In the case of a joke, that moment of apprehension creates laughter.

Jokes are any easy way to illustrate what Koestler means.

Think of the most clichéd joke in the world:

> 'A man walked into a bar and hurt his head. It was an iron bar.'

Once you have picked yourself up off the floor and wiped away those tears of mirth, consider that the idea behind the joke is a verbal misunderstanding: we are led, deliberately, down one path by the teller, only to have the truth revealed at the last moment. The same is true for Henny Youngman's signature line: 'Take my wife – PLEASE!' We laugh because an observation suddenly becomes a plea – punning around the two different meanings of the verb 'to take'.

Children's jokes show the same splitting of focus:

> 'What lies at the bottom of the sea shaking? A nervous wreck.'

> 'What stands in a field and goes "Ooh, ooh"? A cow with no lips.'

A child laughs because they are forced to make a mental leap to connect the two ideas.

The playful comedian

Most comedians would recognize an element of this thinking in their writing. We are there on stage to offer an escape from the everyday world. All comedians do this by playing with an audience, asking them to partake (for 20 minutes, at least) in the comedian's slightly twisted take on reality.

Most adults are encouraged in everyday life (and certainly at work) to behave in a serious 'grown up' way. This means, in general, dealing with one idea at a time; we try to be clear about what we are saying so as not to confuse our listeners. Separate ideas may be linked together, but we are at pains to point out the connections between them.

The comedian, however, finds that the rules are a little less exacting: we are encouraged (and encourage our audience) to compare and contrast different things or behaviour. We may allow ourselves to be dismissive about something that is terribly important or obsess about the inconsequential. In essence, we are allowed to play. This freedom could be viewed as a mini holiday for the audience. As a budding comic, you should embrace this opportunity: they have paid good money to watch you at a comedy club; they *want* to have a good time; they want to be told things they have never considered before, to be lifted out of the mundane world around them. The audience are prepared to go down any path the comedian opens up before them: as long as you keep them laughing, they will follow you wherever you lead them.

What is a joke?

Theories about jokes come and go out of fashion all the time. There is, however, a model that seems to hold true for *most* jokes. A definition, if you will. It is this:

A joke is something that must have all the information implicit in the set up, that when the 'surprise' of the punchline is revealed, it all makes sense.

To return to the oldest joke in the world:

'A man walked into a bar and hurt his head. It was an iron bar.'

It wouldn't work if we said, 'A man walks into a pub'– we have lost the connection. The ambiguity of language, the multiple meanings of some words, hides momentarily the information we need at the end to 'get' it.

Just before you throw this book down in disgust, thinking that all you've done is buy something that teaches you how to understand bad jokes, let me try your patience with one more example that, again, we've heard before:

'What lies at the bottom of the sea, shivering? A nervous wreck.'

Clearly, all the information is there in the set up for us to make the connection. Wrecks have to lie at the bottom of the sea, we can't put it anywhere else to make the joke work. We also have to think of an adjective to denote nervousness. We could say 'What lies at the bottom of the sea *worrying* or *fretting*' but again, it might not have the right degree of ambiguity. 'Shivering' is vague enough to hide the information.

If we are British and we hear a joke involving an Englishman, an Irishman and a Scotsman, we know the joke will probably involve the Englishman being a bit priggish, the Scotsman probably being a bit mean spirited and the Irishman getting completely the wrong end of the stick. Once we understand the hidden ground rules we can let the comic misunderstandings play themselves out with almost endless variation.

Most working comedians don't do something as bald as this when writing. The information hidden in their set ups, which will allow the audience to 'get' the joke, is often supplied by their *attitude* to the material. As has been suggested earlier, the comedian writing about relationships, who is hopelessly in love, is going to write totally different material about relationships from the comic going through a bitter divorce.

So let's take a closer look at attitude.

Attitude, the comedian's secret weapon

How you feel about a subject will dictate how you make it funny

Any idiot can tell a joke. All it takes is good memory and a clear speaking voice.

Professional comedians, these days, rarely tell jokes told in the third person ('Two men on a desert island...'), and they would certainly never tell gags that they've heard before. What the professional comic tends to do is to talk about how they see things and what their *attitude* to it all is. It is personal to *them*.

Do they love the subject they are talking about? Do they hate it? Does it worry them? Does it remind them of something else? In short, how do they *feel* about it?

Attitude is terribly important. In many cases, it can help supply that implicit information that the audience need to 'get' the joke. For instance, Jack Benny built his career on being stingy with money. So much so, that when he was playing a scene on his radio show in which he was being robbed, legend has it that he managed to clock up the longest laugh ever recorded on radio. A mugger, pointing a gun at Benny demands 'Your money or your life!' There is a long pause. The criminal repeats it again, 'Look pal! I said your money or your life!' Benny snaps back: 'I'm thinking it over!'

Jack Dee portrays himself as a miserable moaner. Given this, it is likely that his default position to a subject is likely to be negative (a pretty general state, admittedly) but this negativity might manifest itself in any particular joke as a much more specific attitude; as either disappointment, or world-weariness or being self-serving. He may be thought of as a moaner (the comedian, not the man!) but he is far from being a one-note comedian; his misanthropy can inspire a myriad of attitudes.

Let's take a really positive state: love. How do you feel about it? You probably think it's a good thing, that it gives you a warm fuzzy feeling, that love makes the world go round, and so on. But how do you *really* feel about the subject, when we get down and dirty to the specifics? How do you feel if you suspect your partner loves you more than you love them? Is there a vague feeling of guilt or being put upon tinged with love? How do you feel if you suspect you are more into your partner then they are into you? Desperate? Suspicious? Far too eager to please? Bitter? Used? Suicidal? Just how far do you, as a comedian, want to play it? As far as it takes to get to the best jokes would be the short answer. How do these different mind-sets inform a comedian's material?

We all have an attitude to everything (if we examine ourselves closely enough) and this is what the comedian needs to exploit in order to travel towards the joke. For example, parking restrictions are a terrible thing in a city, but not if you have the correct parking permit and someone (who hasn't got one) can't take your bay. It all depends on your attitude.

An acerbic, angry comic like Jerry Sadowitz will talk about ex-girlfriends in a totally different way from, say, the breezy, optimistic Australian comic Adam Hill. A bird spotter, like 80s comic Johnny Immaterial, presumably wouldn't describe pigeons as 'rats with wings', as Woody Allen once did.

Examples of attitude at work

Here's how a comedian might use different attitudes to explore the same subject in three different ways. In this case, let's stick to the theme of 'love' and play with the attitudes of disappointment, world-weariness and being devious.

Disappointment: I've just fallen in love again... She's not my first choice, but beggars can't be choosers.

World-weariness: I've just fallen in love again... I suppose it'll keep me occupied for a brief while between the cradle and the grave.

Devious: I've just fallen in love again... although to tell you the truth, I'm only going out with her so I can sleep with her best friend.

By pursuing a specific attitude, we find that we are half way towards a joke.

This may mean that the comedian needs to wear their heart on their sleeve a little more when they are on stage then when they are off. They need to tell the audience how they feel about things, which means, often as not, that not only must they play a more extreme attitude to the subject matter than they would in real life, they must also show us more clearly exactly how they feel about it. Their attitude must be clear to the audience, otherwise how will they be able to guess the intent of the comic? The message must be clear. And, unlike a badly told joke in a pub, mood matters.

Attitude games

A letter of hate

(A solo writing game)

Write a letter to someone or some institution that you really hate, congratulating them for everything they have done for you and the rest of the world. The more specific you allow the detail to become, the more information you will have to get your teeth into. It doesn't have to be about an 'important' matter (although if a government's lack of action on global warming annoys you, get writing!). It could be a very petty subject, like congratulating a manager for the poor service you received in their shop or a restaurant, or the traffic warden for being such a stickler for detail and giving you a ticket.

This game offers you the guise of pretending to praise something, when in actual fact you are sticking the knife in and twisting it. As such, it works on two creative levels: the comic is practising the valuable skill of saying one thing while revealing another and (perhaps equally importantly) we are learning to use our anger as an engine of creativity. Sometimes, if we are too angry about a subject it can be very difficult to address it in comedy terms; we just end up shouting at our audience. Or worse, we start lecturing them. But by approaching the subject from an oblique angle (praising something we dislike), we can sometimes harness that rage in a way that helps us attack what specifically we hate about the subject.

For example, I think we all probably find the terms 'collateral damage' or 'friendly fire' very distasteful euphemisms for killing people. They attempt to sanitize something that is quite horrific – pain, suffering and extinction. Human bodies reduced to smoking meat. But what if the writer of the letter is congratulating the politician or military spokesperson trying to whitewash all this death? Perhaps the writer thinks this is right because we shouldn't frighten sensitive people with something as sordid as the truth. What other truths should be hidden from the sensitive public? The writer should make some suggestions. Perhaps, by logical extension, all signs of pain and suffering should be removed from the public's eye? Anyone with an infirmity must be incarcerated to prevent upsetting the public. Perhaps all historical battles should be re-branded so they don't sound so dangerous. The 'Gun Fight at the OK Corral' could now be called the 'Bun Fight at the OK Corral'. Much cosier. Perhaps the writer could suggest other 'cuddly' terms for death and destruction?

This application of extreme forms of logic divorced from humanity can be a perfect tool for the satirical comedian to use. Think of Jonathan Swift's *A Modest Proposal*, where he suggests the Irish eat their own children as a solution to the growing famine.

The writer can go from impotent outrage at the stupidity of others to actually addressing the issue and making an audience deal with it. Needless to say, it is a writing game that can be played again and again to unlock material.

Write a letter as an extreme personality

(A solo writing game)

Think about the type of person you hate the most and then write another letter as if you were that person. You could be writing as an extreme racist defending someone's zero immigration policy; you could be an ultra liberal ex-hippy saying that not only should drugs should be decriminalized, but that they should be made compulsory as well.

This is a different game from the previous hate letter because this time you are writing as a completely different character from yourself. Millions of different voices inhabit our brain through the course of our lives, even ones that seem horrible or hateful to us. They must exist somewhere inside us for us to be able to create them. In this game, you are just training yourself to listen to some of these more extreme ones. You may find this incredibly liberating. You may find that, once you have the parameters of the character clearly thought out, the material seems to be writing itself. If it does, then you may find yourself beginning to create a character act.

If the letter seems to be stagnating or to have gone off the boil a bit, ask yourself whether you can push the extremes of the character even more or whether you are being specific enough in your subject matter. Always hone in on your topic and always push the attitudes more.

Obsessive detail

(A solo writing game)

Write about a hobby you enjoy as if you were a foaming mouth fanatic; write about it in such detail that if you were telling people about it out loud, they would back away from you slowly, trying not to make any sudden movements. What does this extreme version of you think about people who don't share this hobby? How would you as a fanatic treat them? How would your entire life revolve around this subject? How would your every waking hour be governed by it?

Compliment/insult game

(A group activity)

Sit in a circle and go round, one by one, complimenting the person to your left. All the compliments must be specific – choose one thing about them only and don't be vague. For example, talk about their eyes rather than general things you feel about them. Being specific is very important! Each person complimented must say 'thank you' before they turn to the left to give their compliment.

Once everyone has had a turn, go round a second time – but this time take that same piece of information used in the compliment and turn it into an insult. Again the recipient of the insult has to say 'thank you' before it's their turn.

Often the results of this exercise can be very funny. Perhaps because the people in the group feel let off the hook, they feel able to say whatever they want. It is understood that there is no personal animosity in this game; if there were, it wouldn't be as funny.

It's often funny because we remember the compliment and we're waiting to hear how it's twisted into an insult. The players are mirroring a traditional joke structure of the set up (the compliment) and the punchline (the insult). So the compliment 'You have a lovely smile' transforms to 'If I had teeth like that, love, I wouldn't show them off...' the second time around. Or 'You were the first person in the group to say hello to me' becomes, in the insult round: 'Stop stalking me, you're creeping me out!' It's not yet a joke structure, but it is getting the recipients used to thinking more like a comic.

This exercise forces the players to look at something specific from two completely different angles: 'I love it' and 'I hate it.' The players can see, by their examples and (perhaps more importantly), by the examples of the other people in the group how opposite attitudes can change the perspective on one simple subject. As such, this exercise is a very good indicator of what we mean by 'attitude'.

building a joke

In this chapter you will learn:
- some common themes in helping a comedian approach material
- why the afterthought is essential to a joke
- some joke writing games.

We've all got one 'funny' uncle who bores us to death with the same jokes every Christmas and family get-together. The big thing that separates professional comedians from amateurs is *authorship*. **We all write our own material.** We don't steal, we don't appropriate and we don't recycle thinly disguised jokes that we have read off the Internet. Previous generations of comedians may have shared gags, but we write our own. We're more like singer-songwriters than a crooner who sings cover versions: Bob Dylan rather than Frank Sinatra.

Of course, most modern comedians don't tell 'jokes' in the traditional sense of the word. What they do is share their ideas with the audience. The comedian 'talks to' an audience rather than the funny uncle who 'talks at'. The comic allows free rein to some of the more extreme aspects of his or her personality and hopes that this 'voice' will generate funny ideas. Almost invariably they have an attitude to their subject, and it is this attitude that generates humour. In essence:

Extreme attitudes to specific points can lead to humour

Comedians may think something's a stupid idea (for example, doing nothing about global warming) and decide to turn it on its head. Like a Nick Revell gag where, pretending to be a style guru, he spoke of the plus side of rising sea levels; how it would get rid of 'untidy' and 'unstylish' low-lying areas like Bangladesh or Norfolk.

Or a comic may love something as a concept and wonder why it can't be replicated in other areas of life. For example, if Mexican waves cheer up crowds why don't we do them at funerals?

Or perhaps the subject just gets them thinking. For example, when a girlfriend/boyfriend breaks up by saying to you 'It's not you, it's me...', surely what they really mean is 'It *is* you. I find you boring/whinging/psychotically deranged...'

You could say that each of those potential jokes revolves around three different methods of approach.

Approach 1: The wrong attitude for the situation

This first approach is self-explanatory – we can all think of things we hate and why. If the audience agree with you, they'll want to hear more. If your *attitude* to the subject is petty, spiteful, selfish or just wrongheaded then you're probably one step nearer to getting a laugh. For example, you may tell the audience that you are against global warming – not because of the environmental impact, but because you get an irritating rash in hot weather.

Approach 2: Misunderstanding

The second example (why is it unacceptable to perform Mexican waves at funerals?) is playing with the concept of 'If this is such a good idea in *this* situation, why won't it work in *that* situation?' The comedian is pretending to misunderstand, for comic effect, our choices of behaviour. Right action, wrong situation. It is applying a comedian's logic to a situation, such as the old joke: 'If black box flight recorders always survive airplane crashes, why don't they just build the whole aeroplane out of the same stuff they make the black box out of?'

Approach 3: Revealing the horrible truth...

The final example (how your boyfriend/girlfriend might try to let you down gently) is playing with the idea of what people say and what they really mean. In effect we are blurting out the unpalatable truth, which we would rather sugarcoat, in order to get a laugh.

But what each joke is really attempting to do is to say, in a funny way, that which usually remains unsaid. But the desire to say the socially unacceptable comment doesn't have to be the only impetus for the comedian's craft. Here are some other common underlying currents found in the comedian's writing:

- I love it.
- We all love this because... (insert comedian's logic)
- I hate it.
- We all hate it because...
- Let's look at it from this angle...

- What if the next step was…?
- Why do we do this?
- What we should do is…
- How does that work?

Always ask yourself: 'What is the comedian's answer to this particular problem?'

The comedian is usually, on some level, trying to find an answer to a problem. It may not be the best answer, or the most socially responsible, but it is *their* answer.

Robert Graves was once asked what he thought the point of poetry was. He answered that a poem was the poet's answer to a particular problem. Rather like an oyster being irritated by a piece of grit and producing a beautiful, lustrous pearl around it; then similarly, a poet produces a beautiful web of images around their particular 'gritty' problem. It may not be the most realistic answer, but it is the answer that suits the poet's purpose best. That seems to be a very good definition of the comedian's craft: we are building up a joke around a particular problem that we perceive. This is true whether that problem revolves around something simple, like a word having two different meanings, as in the old joke: 'I went to the butchers to buy some bacon. He said "Lean back?" So I leant back.' Or Harry Hill's word-play gag: 'I took my step-ladder. Not my *real* ladder.' It is also true if the problem trying to be resolved is as huge as religion. Here's George Carlin on theology:

> 'Think about it. Religion has actually convinced people that there's an invisible man – living in the sky – who watches everything you do, every minute of every day. And the invisible man has a special list of ten things he does not want you to do. And if you do any of these ten things, he has a special place, full of fire and smoke and burning and torture and anguish, where he will send you to live and suffer and burn and choke and scream and cry forever and ever 'til the end of time! But He loves you.'

George Carlin, *'You Are all Diseased'*, 1999

So always ask yourself: 'What is the *best* comic answer to this particular problem?'

A joke, therefore, can arise out of addressing specific problems (not vague ones – know your target!). It will often be fuelled by the comedian's attitude to the subject. In Carlin's example above, this is his contempt for the logic of organized religion.

To put it crudely:

SPECIFIC SUBJECT + ATTITUDE = COMIC'S SOLUTION (OR JOKE)

Finding the joke

What we need to complete the equation is some sort of editorializing point or remark to supply the laugh. This is what supplies the punchline. In the case of comedienne Mary Bourke, the joke becomes:

> 'I never shop at Primark. I can't help thinking of all those blind Korean orphans asleep over their sewing machines. A tear in every stitch. 'Cause the tears make the leather very supple.'

In the case of Nick Revell the subject matter becomes:

> 'There are shocking rates of illiteracy and innumeracy in this country. Children are becoming more and more stupid. Whereas in the Far East, not only can they read and write, they can also make really good sportswear, fake Gap jeans, real Gap jeans, trainers, sportswear... They're not lying around the house playing computer games and getting fat on junk food – they're doing 12-hour shifts in sweatshops at the age of five – making something of their lives.'

Both comedians are being specific and highlighting an attitude, but what generates the laugh is the *afterthought* that they provide. The afterthought is often the mechanism the comedian uses for generating a laugh, and it is what we shall now turn our attention to.

Afterthoughts

Afterthoughts are almost always the reason why we laugh at a comedian's routine. If the first thought is the set up, the afterthought can be thought of as the punchline. The afterthought is the line that supplies the other half of the joke equation. Really, it is a less daunting way for the new comedian to define a punchline.

Afterthoughts are something that most of us are trained to use in everyday life. We may use them in the workplace (managers might use them to show that they are not some inhuman tyrant); we could supply some self-deprecating comment at a party to show we aren't 'really' bragging about our job or status; or we might add a silly afterthought to a comment on a first date to broadcast, in an unconscious way of course, what a witty and funny individual we are and how much it would be worth getting to know us better.

Afterthoughts are everywhere. Any time that you are offering a qualification or commenting on something you or someone else has said, or any time you add a sarcastic comment to something particularly stupid that someone else has said, then you are exercising your afterthought ability.

This is often precisely what a comedian is doing when they make an audience laugh.

To be absolutely clear, an afterthought is a continuation of the previous thought; it is *not* a contradiction. So for instance, the statement 'We've been married 25 years now' can be followed up by the afterthought 'and it's time to tell you I only did it for a bet.' But a straight contradiction of 'No we haven't' would make no sense at all. An afterthought continues the initial thought and takes it in a different direction.

If you look at the jokes quoted in this book, most of them rely on the afterthought to generate the laugh.

Sometimes the afterthought can be supplied with just a look from the comic, in the form of a raised eyebrow or a mugging to the audience. Sometimes the afterthought is supplied by showing a different emotion from the one the words would have us believe (like saying you are really pleased for someone else's success through gritted teeth and trying not to choke on the words). But an afterthought should always aim to take the audience by surprise. It is a thought that comes out of the blue, but that still has a twisted logic about it.

Encourage your afterthoughts

Sometimes you can add an afterthought to an afterthought. Try to encourage yourself to do this (at least when you are writing) because it is an excellent way of opening out material. If you add an afterthought to an initial thought and the audience laugh, then you have written a joke; but if you add another afterthought to that first one, then qualify that thought with another afterthought, before making an editorial point to *that* afterthought, before clarifying your thought one degree further, then you are well on your way to writing a routine. At the very least you will have given yourself a fair chance at exploring the subject matter and exploring your attitude to the subject.

Examples of afterthought gags

Definitive statements are quite good for generating afterthoughts, as are broad general statements that require a comedian's qualification on the subject. Here are, at random, some general ideas that comedians have played the afterthought game with over the past 20 years:

- I've been married five times...
- I don't believe in Astrology...
- Ethnic minorities – they're not like us!
- I think you should get to know someone properly when you start dating them...

These definitive statements have been qualified by various comedians to become:

- 'I've been married five times. Every one a success!' (aging lothario Ronnie Rigsby, mistaking quantity for quality)
- 'I don't believe in Astrology. But then again I'm a Capricorn and they're naturally very sceptical.' (Nick Revell)
- 'Dad said, "Remember son, those ethnic minorities – they're not like us!" I said, "I know Dad. Some of them have jobs."' (Steve Hall)
- 'I think a person should get to know someone and even be in love with them before you use them and degrade them.' (Steve Martin)

So when thinking about jokes, bear the following model in mind:

Specific thought leads to unexpected afterthought.

Afterthought games

Listed below are some afterthought exercises. Remember the following when you try them:

- You are allowed to be incredibly flippant or say the inappropriate thing, so don't edit yourself.
- Try to get used to saying the first attitude that pops into your head.
- Don't worry about being impolite or rude. For the rest of your comedy career you will be exercising, in one way or another, your ability to throw thoughts out into the void and catching whatever twisted afterthoughts you can to make a joke.

Positive/negative

Write down some banal, happy thoughts. For once, we don't have to be specific: general statements will do. In the case of this exercise, the blander, the better. Lines like: 'Aren't summers lovely?', 'The weekend's coming around!' or 'The birds are singing sweetly in the tree' are perfect for our purposes.

Then put those thoughts away in a drawer for at least a day before returning to look at them again.

On this second viewing, try to add very negative afterthoughts that twist the original thought in a different area. It cannot be stressed enough that all thoughts of propriety or 'niceness' must be checked at the door. You must give yourself licence to write whatever afterthoughts you want for the purpose of this game. Remember to kill your internal social editor!

For example, the previous day you might have written: 'I like children' and today you might supply the afterthought (as W.C. Fields did) 'but I couldn't eat a whole one' or 'they're much easier to beat at kick boxing'.

The thought 'I love chicken!' could have tagged on to it the following day 'that's why I married one!' or 'but I prefer the taste of human flesh'.

This is a great game for providing a workout for the brain. It trains the aspiring comedian to exercise those comedy muscles; and the more you stretch them, the stronger they will become.

Eventually you won't need a day away from the initial thoughts to come up with something twisted; you'll be able to say something incredibly flippant as soon as the first thought comes out of your mouth.

Subverting proverbs

Write down some old proverbs or sayings then provide an afterthought that tweaks them in a completely different direction.

So, instead of saying 'Red sky at night, shepherd's delight', we might change it to 'Red sky at night, my house is on fire'. Or 'Red sky at night, World War Three has begun'.

'Too many cooks spoil the broth' might become 'Too many cooks are on TV'.

The nice thing about this game is that all these sayings are embedded in the popular consciousness, so they have a dull familiarity that we can capitalize on, so that the 'rug-pull' surprise of your subversion will doubly delight.

This game can be set up as a group game, with each comic shouting out his or her own proverb and everyone trying to top the last person's particular afterthought gag. Don't be shy of reincorporating earlier ideas (for example, if someone offered 'Red sky in the morning' then expect some wag to add on 'My house is *still* on fire!').

Subverting memes

According to Richard Dawkins, a meme is any unit of information that passes from mind to mind. It could be an irritating tune, a song lyric, an over-used phrase (for example '24/7'), a catchphrase or an advertising slogan. A lot of them sit like unwanted junk mail in your brain. If so, this exercise is your opportunity to exorcise these particular demons. It is time to do your own thinking, rather than let the meme do the thinking for us. (And if you think that is an overstatement then ask yourself why we all feel maudlin when we hear a sad song on the radio.)

Instead of the proverbs of the previous game (which, come to think of it, are cultural memes, too), you have to add twisted afterthoughts to whatever memes you are using. Let's start with advertising slogans because they are easy targets. The old slogan 'A Mars a day helps you work, rest and play' can easily become, for our purposes: 'A Mars a day helps you work, rest and become diabetic'.

Remember the advertising jingle of the 70s and 80s that went:

'A million housewives every day

Pick up a can of beans and say

"Beanz! Meanz! Heinz!"'

That could easily be subverted into:

'A million housewives every day

Pick up a can of beans and say

"Why am I making such poor food choices for my children?"'

Of course, it doesn't just have to be an advert; memes crop up everywhere. Think about bad literary devices. The writer and comedienne Sheila Hyde used to have a line in her set parodying Mills and Boon styles:

'He wasn't attractive in the conventional sense of the word. Or, indeed, in any sense of the word.'

Her afterthought was poking fun at a cultural meme. The clunking, conversational clichés that add nothing to our lives are also memes and can easily be lampooned with afterthoughts:

'At the end of the day... the sun sets.'

So think of different categories of memes and attempt to add afterthoughts that twist or undercut them. If it makes you laugh or smile then it's probably worth trying it out in front of a live audience.

The eternal optimist

This is almost a straight reversal of the 'Positive/Negative' game. Think of really horrible, negative statements, then try to add some sort of positive spin to the situation. So the statement 'The doctors have only given me six months to live' could be countered with 'Pretty cool for a may fly!' or 'Luckily I live in Doncaster, so it will seem much longer...'

It is, for some reason, a much harder exercise than that of putting a negative spin on an initial positive thought, but it is worth persevering with. Often a lovely, silly energy can come out of the afterthoughts generated.

The best of times, the worst of times

Write down as many aspirations as you can think of and be sure to be quite specific. It would not be enough to write 'I want to be the richest person in the world'; you would need to detail how rich you would be and what you would do with that wealth. Try to be specific! Once you have written these aspirations, return to the list and try to imagine the flip side of that thought, the worst possible fear that you have concerning wealth or beauty or power or whatever the first fantasy was based on. But ensure that the two thoughts relate to each other. Remember, a joke must have all the information in the set up so that when the punchline is revealed, the audience can make a connection. That is why the first thought should be specific rather than general, so that your brain has some material to play with for the returning negative thought.

Here's a short version of this game:

> 'I want to have the body of Matt Damon. But I'm frightened that I have the body of Matt Lucas.'

A more surreal version might be:

> 'I want to have the body of Matt Damon. And, luckily, I win his body in a raffle... but unfortunately I have to wait until after his death before I can collect it...'

Here's a longer version of this game:

(To show the value of being specific, we must look at a very detailed set up to this game.)

> 'I want to die in my bed after a full and happy life, surrounded by all my surviving ex-lovers weeping in gratitude for having known me, with all my successful and adoring children smiling through tears in celebration of my parenting skills. Outside a throng of people hold a candle light vigil, singing songs to ease my passing. As I feel the final moment approaching I lean forward and say something so profound about life that it becomes the basis of a new philosophy that radically alters human nature for the better.

> 'What I will probably get is to die on a sofa bed in my bedsit in early middle age after a long and protracted embarrassing illness which makes me look slightly ridiculous. I am surrounded by ex-lovers, ex-wives and

children who are there to squabble over who gets what when I die. Every time I ask for a glass of water, they punch me and tell me to stop interrupting them. Outside a throng of people approach holding firebrands screaming 'Let's burn the evil pig!' They are my many creditors, demanding blood. As I feel my final moment approach I wee a bit in fear and try to say something proud, but as I lean forward my false teeth fall out, slurring my speech (which I'd stolen from a 'Hallmark' condolences card) and no one hears me anyway because 'Celebrity Fat Farm' has just started on TV. I am buried in an unmarked grave, on unhallowed ground, with a spike through my heart.'

Always be specific!

Being specific allows you to reincorporate or refer back to earlier references, but this time giving them a different 'spin'. The key to this game is to think of your absolute highest wish and then contrast it with your worst possible fear. We laugh because the comedian is mining a public paranoia. We are all secretly terrified that the worst will happen to us and this game helps to bring those fears into the open and lets us laugh at them. It can be a collective exorcism.

This exercise is, obviously, a great way for the comedian to practise playing with contrasting attitudes. The more you exercise those comedy muscles, the stronger they can become. But you can also craft jokes out of this game. The actress and comedienne Alyssa Kyria wrote a great joke from this exercise that always gets a laugh:

'You know, I don't ask much from a relationship, ladies and gentlemen. All I want is earth-shattering sex that lasts for hours and hours, a champagne breakfast in the morning and to bask in a warm afterglow, but what I usually get is – sore.'

It is a delightful rug-pull that takes the audience unaware.

When I say that, what I really mean is...

Write down some bland statements and then begin to qualify them. Then qualify those qualifications. Repeat until you run out of steam. The trick is to get specific, then elaborate on that particular detail. Feel free to go off at mad tangents, but always make sure that you are referring to the previous statement.

Here are some conversational clichés off the top of my head:

- 'I really like you.'
- 'Is it cold in here?'
- 'Merry Christmas, everyone!'

Now, let's see if we can qualify these thoughts into the ground:

- **'I really like you,** and when I say that, what I really mean is that you'll do until someone really interesting comes along, or at least someone with proper fitting dentures who knows how to kiss. Don't get me wrong, you're the most interesting 90-year-old I've ever gone out with. I'm just looking for someone that I have more in common with. Like another man. I'm not gay – it's just that it would be cheaper if I lived with another man to bulk buy razor blades...'

- **'Is it cold in here,** or is it me? It's probably me, I've just come back from a two-year holiday in the tropics. Well, I say 'holiday' – in actual fact the last 18 months were spent in a Thai Prison. That'll teach me to punch a local policeman. I didn't mean to, I was aiming for the nun standing next to him. Well, I say nun, she was wearing one of those wimples, so I suppose she could have been in a hen party. Prison was quite exotic, if you've never experienced true despair before. Cockroaches, dysentery and the ever-present threat of violence: I could've just as easily taken a trip to Margate and saved myself the airfare. And the tattoos...'

- **'Merry Christmas, everyone!** Well, I say, everyone. Obviously, not you Grandad. I've never forgiven you for not getting me a tank last year. I didn't even want a real one (well, I did – but I don't think it would have fitted under the tree...). A simple toy one would have done. Admittedly, I was 28 at the time, but I don't see why kids should have all the fun. It's wasted on them anyway – that's why I made my children dig coal until their 18th birthday...'

You may find that jokes arise from this approach. But even if they don't, persevere! It is an invaluable exercise for making you pursue a specific idea to illogical extremes. For the purposes of this exercise the journey is much more important than the ending. You are training your brain to come up with endless afterthoughts. You are also learning that you can always get even more specific on any given topic; like an onion, you can always peel off one more layer of meaning.

A British comedian Trevor Lock has almost elevated this approach to an art form. He starts his set by saying:

'Hello. My name is Trevor Lock and I'm from the future. I'm not. Well, I am. But I'm only from next Tuesday.' (He'd look down at himself.) 'This is what we're wearing next Tuesday. It's not. It's what *I'm* wearing next Tuesday. And today.'

He would sometimes stretch out these contradictions and elaborations for well over half his set.

03

comedy
ground rules

In this chapter you will learn:
- how to squeeze a joke out of almost any subject
- how to turn off your social editor
- why your writing should be concise and to the point.

Here are some points that you may wish to consider at the outset.

Style or content?

This is more a question than a ground rule. Which end of the spectrum do you think is most important? Obviously, material is very important, but if the comedian has no stage presence, then what chance is there that the audience will listen to the joke? The best joke in the world has to be delivered to a crowd. Conversely, if the comic is all style and no substance then the audience is going to feel cheated when his or her confidence isn't backed up by solid material.

Clearly, both style and content are vital for the comedian. If you have no ability to convey your set to an audience, if you are incapable of presenting us with an attitude that illustrates what the joke is about, then perhaps you might consider the career of comedy writer rather than comedy performer.

Kill little Mr/Ms social control in your head

Many people, when asked why they would never consider performing stand-up comedy, say that they would be too frightened. It *is* a scary business. It takes guts, initially, to stand-up in front of a group of strangers and try to entertain them. Just ask anyone who has had to deliver a seminar at work or a speech at a wedding. This type of fear we can recognize as stage fright.

But there is another type of fear that also governs us all, whether we are performers or not; it is much more pervasive in our lives and it is definitely not helpful to the comedian. It is the social fear that says things like: 'I can't wear *that* to work' or 'I'd better not say *that* in front of my elders' or 'I'm too old to dress like that'. It is the type of fear that tries to rein us in so we are always on our best behaviour. It is the little social controller that lives in your head that is obsessed with trying to make you blend in with the herd. It is the part of your brain that tells you to conform because you don't want people to think that you are a bit strange. Often this internal editor can stifle our ideas before we have had a chance to fully explore them. We feel that our thoughts are not good enough, or too clichéd or a bit clumsy;

this in turn, makes *us* feel a bit clichéd or a bit clumsy or that we are simply not good enough. In extreme cases, we become incredibly self-conscious and grind to a halt.

The way that this social controller manifests itself in comics is they edit themselves out of the game before they have even started by saying things like:

- 'My joke is too obvious.'
- 'Why bother? Bill Hicks covered this subject ten years ago – and he did it much better than me.'
- 'I don't think the audience will get this material, it's just peculiar to me.'
- 'The audience won't want to hear me talk about *that*.'

This kind of thinking puts a block on our brains. We cease to play. Instead of metaphorically saying 'yes, and...' to new ideas we find ourselves saying 'no, but...' All the social controller does is close down our options.

So, a more constructive way of looking at these four worries might be to answer them thus:

- 'My joke is too obvious.' How do you know if you haven't tried it out? It may be obvious in hindsight because you, the author, have already made that connection. The audience have yet to make that journey.
- 'Why bother? Bill Hicks covered this subject ten years ago – and he did it much better than me.' This may be true – but you have never covered it before. Your insights and attitudes (trust me) will be different.
- I don't think the audience will get this material, it's just peculiar to me.' By this, sometimes a comedian will mean that they think the audience is too stupid to get it, sometimes they are assuming that the audience will be ignorant of the experience; either way they are assuming that the audience is incapable of understanding. This could be construed as being a little patronizing. My answer to this sort of whinge would be: 'What makes you so special?' Other people have shared most experiences, so you should have some people in the audience who are receptive to it. But even if your worst fears were right, how will you know unless you try out the idea?
- 'The audience won't want to hear me talk about *that*.' Once more, you are trying to second-guess what you think the audience want you to hear. Rather in the same way that we might try not to be too rude in front of Granny, forgetting the

fact that she was once our age, has lived a full life, has probably cursed once or twice, as well as having seen people born and watched people die, we make decisions on what we think is 'right' or 'proper' for our audience to hear.

The social controller sitting on your shoulder would have you believe that the world is scrutinizing you, just waiting for you to trip up, but the liberating reality is that *no one cares*. They just want you to be funny. The part of you that tries to be polite and say the right thing is probably not the most interesting aspect of your psyche. The audience want the part of you that takes risks, that ruffles feathers, that says the unspoken thought. You could take some cold comfort in the fact that they would rather you go down with all guns blazing than be timid and 'play safe'. So don't edit out your thoughts before you have had a chance to explore them.

Remember

People will eventually be paying you money to behave like an idiot, so start behaving like one (on stage, obviously). Learn to say the socially awkward thing. State the blindingly obvious. Play the fool. Then watch how the sky hasn't fallen or how your friends don't desert you and how, quite possibly, you have made the audience laugh.

Practise saying (or thinking) the inappropriate thing to say on any given situation and watch your little social controller slowly starve to death.

Learn to be flippant.

Stupid name game

Here's an exercise that may help show you how unproductive our social editor can be.

(A group activity but, at a pinch, could be done alone.)

Write down a list of stupid names. They don't have to be funny or clever, just stupid. They can be real names, made up ones, imaginary music hall acts' names, porn stars, soap characters, whatever takes your fancy. The most important thing is not to think about them – just write them down. The pen should never hover above the paper. If it does, write down 'Mr Writer's Block' or 'Penny My Brain Has Dried' or whatever addresses the situation. Give yourself a time limit of two minutes.

When you are done, read out clearly (with no explanations or apologies) your favourite name on the list. Once everyone has read out their favourite name, go round the group again and each read out your least favourite name (but give it the same commitment that you gave the first one).

You will all probably find that there was no noticeable difference in response between what you thought was your best idea and your worst idea. Your worst name may even have got a bigger response. You may find that the clever pun-based names get a lukewarm response, but the really stupid nonsense names illicit big laughs.

The point to learn from this game is that you are not always the best judge of knowing what the audience want to hear, so why edit yourselves before people have had a chance to judge your stuff?

N.B. If you are working alone, write out your list and make a mental note of what you think is your best name and your worst one, then give it to friends and ask them to choose their favourite and least favourite. This is not quite as good as reading them out (stand-up is after all a spoken medium) but you might feel a bit stupid eyeballing someone and reading out a list of names. I guarantee that if you show the list to enough people they will manage to select every name on it.

What's your attitude to the subject?

This should be fairly self-explanatory from what was said about attitude in Chapter 02. But, to reiterate, how do you really feel about a subject? How would you feel about the same subject if you were someone who was timid? Self obsessed? A megalomaniac? Overly polite?

In short, what is your 'take' on a subject?

If you don't have a perspective then the audience will not know which direction you are taking them in.

Learn to look at subjects from as many different angles as possible to unlock the potential joke.

More attitude games

On the plus side/negative side

Write down a list of things off the top of your head. It can be as uncreative and boring as this one that I've just come up with:

- Cats
- Dogs
- Men
- Women
- Houses
- Trees
- The sun

Then write out a plus point about each of them. Make sure you are being really positive and that what you write matters to you. There is no point in being lukewarm about a subject. Here are my plus points:

- Cats: Can be trained to use litter boxes.
- Dogs: Keen to be your friend.
- Men: Very good at putting up shelves.
- Women: Blessed with the communication gene.
- Houses: Somewhere to shelter from a storm.
- Trees: Their branches provide rest for all the lovely birds and their beautiful chorus of birdsong.
- The sun: Source of all heat and life on Planet Earth.

Once you are happy with those thoughts, return to the list and add a negative afterthought exploring a less than happy attitude to the subject, like this:

- Cats: Can be trained to use litter boxes. (Hooray! My house reeks of crap!)
- Dogs: Keen to be your friend. (Too keen. Sometimes they want to take that friendship to the next level and hump your leg.)
- Men: Very good at putting up shelves. (Very good at starting wars.)
- Women: Blessed with the communication gene. (And don't they go on and on about it...)
- Houses: Somewhere to shelter from a storm. (Not so handy for sheltering from an earthquake, though...)

- Trees: Their branches provide rest for all the lovely birds and their beautiful chorus of birdsong. (But not at 5.30 in the morning! What ever happened to bird flu…?)
- The sun: Source of all heat and life on planet Earth. (And skin cancer.)

I think these statements are well on their way to becoming jokes. And it has all come about through the application of differing attitudes. From having gone from quite an unpromising list of very general subjects, it has become a specific list of 'attitude-y' statements.

Seven deadly sins

You don't have to use the seven deadly sins as a template; you could use a trite phrase like 'faith, hope and charity' or 'blood, sweat and tears' or the names of the seven dwarves. Anything that has a list of categories for you to play with will do.

Write down a list of things that you do. It could be anything.

- I like to walk to work.
- Every Tuesday night I do the food shopping.
- My job is to pick up the kids from school.

Then, apply each one of the deadly sins (or whatever other categories you have chosen) to it in turn. For example:

1 (Avarice) I like to walk to work – I love the fact I'm saving 80p on the bus fare, but I worry about the shoe leather I'm using up. Perhaps I should go barefoot?
2 (Sloth) I'd *like* to walk to work – but I just can't be bothered, maybe if I slip my partner a quid they can piggyback me to the office.
3 (Pride) I like to walk to work – it gives me a chance to shout 'Good Morning, Scum' at all the lesser beings. The only drawback is I have to smell their unwashed bodies.
4 (Gluttony) I like to walk to work – I pass three cake shops on my way, and even though they are not open yet, I like to lick the windows and pretend.
5 (Anger) I like to walk to work – WALK! Do you hear me? Not dawdle, you old age pensioner. Now get out of the way before I push you and your Zimmer frame into the road!

6 (Lust) I like to walk to work – then I can saunter up behind people I fancy and look at their bottoms without them noticing.

7 (Envy) I like to walk to work – who am I kidding? I want to drive – sod the environment. I want one of those turbo-charged boy racer cars that my neighbour has, all chrome and fuel injected. I want to be sitting in one of his big plush, leatherette bucket seats, rather than standing here, waiting for the lights to change and choking on his fumes as he thunders by.

This is a game you can return to again and again, and it is particularly useful in training yourself to explore differing attitudes.

Be specific

When writing, learn to focus in on what you really want to address. Try not to make general statements; instead hone in on a specific area of the topic. This will give you something to get your teeth into and it can help you uncover new areas that you wouldn't initially have thought of.

Let's say you want to write about 'friendship'. You might write down that word on a blank piece of A4 and then stare blankly for the next half hour as all your thoughts dissolve into a vague soup of generalities. Then you would crumple up the paper, claiming that there is nothing funny in that area.

But let's try getting specific.

What sort of friendship are we talking about? Best mates at school? Competitive friends? Drinking buddies? Friends who take advantage of you? Friends that you only see out of a sense of duty? Friends of the opposite sex who you really want to be more than friends? Each of these deserves to be treated as separate topics rather than the amorphous general heading that you made up the first time. The subject becomes easier to explore.

How would you behave to a friend that you were seeing out of a sense of duty? Would it be different from the way you behaved with a competitive friend? Would you banter less, perhaps, and patronize more? What jobs would you give a responsible friend that you wouldn't give a drinking buddy? What could you expect to happen to that particular job if your party animal friend took it over? Would 'Mr Party Animal' be the best person to organize your mother's funeral, for example?

I hope you are beginning to see how, by learning to be specific, we are spicing up a potentially bland subject. Indeed, I hope we are beginning to see that there is no such thing as a boring subject.

When teaching comedy I often give people specific lists for homework, so they can get stuck into something without having to worry if the subject that they have chosen is 'old hat' or bland. I ask them to be specific, but every so often a student will come back with a really general list. I might ask them to come up with a list of things that they think are important, and they might write down things like: dogs, cats, clouds, sunny days, love, happiness, truth, justice... These ideas are so general as to almost have no meaning. Generalities very rarely lead to jokes because generalities very rarely lead anywhere.

So, when writing, don't write 'I like football', when what you mean is 'I like *watching* football' or more specifically, 'I like watching football on the TV and hurling abuse at the screen because, on some quantum level, I believe the players can hear me and that my advice, as a grossly overweight man who was always picked last in school teams, will obviously be better than the footballers' instinct as multi-millionaire athletes.'

The beautiful thing about being specific is that it is almost an infinite process. There is always another layer of the subject to be unpeeled. Marry that with exploring different attitudes, and the comedian has an almost limitless engine of creativity at their disposal.

Games to develop specific thinking

Lateralization

Write down the subject you wish to explore (and be specific!) in the middle of a large piece of paper. Using arrows, subheadings or even diagrams, start writing down everything you can think of that relates to this subject, no matter how deranged it may seem – this is your piece of paper, it's just an exploration, no one else is ever going to see it. Then start scribbling down associations to the first series of associations. Keep branching out, making strange connections and associations with the original subject matter until the paper is full. Feel free to play with different attitudes and emotions too. Are there any strange connections that you can see, any possible jokes that are uncovered? Even if there aren't, it's not a bad exercise for just exercising your creative muscles.

Falling in love with an object

(A solo and group activity)

I'm very grateful to fellow comedian and comedy lecturer Huw Thomas for showing me this exercise when we were working together at Middlesex University.

This can be treated as a written or a performance game. If it's the latter you may want to record what you are saying in case something funny occurs. If you are treating it as a writing game, try really hard to push your emotional extremes on paper.

The idea is to pick on some physical object and to start enthusing about every aspect of it. Start small (i.e. only mildly pleased to start with) and build slowly to a point where you have become hopelessly enamoured with the thing. Single out individual characteristics and what makes them each so brilliant. Why is its shape so good? What feelings does it evoke in you? What are the surfaces like? Be incredibly specific. Once you have worked yourself into a frenzy, try to discover the object's one fatal flaw that makes the thing less than perfect. Focus on this and, rather like a jilted lover, start finding other reasons for hating this object. How could you have been so stupid to be fooled? It's obviously sub-standard – explain how you were wrong initially and how stupid you were to be taken in by its cheap, tawdry surface appeal. The trick to this game is to be as extreme as you possibly can in both praising and damning the object, but always focus on specific things. (Note: If you are performing this exercise in front of people, they should be left in no doubt that you are massively over-reacting to what is, after all, only an inanimate object. The more obsessive or emotional that you can become about a piece of furniture or stationery (for example), then the more rewarding the experience will probably be.) The whole experience should be fuelled by the two things that help comedians create jokes: being specific and playing with attitude. This game should force you to get used to looking at seemingly banal everyday things in more and more detail and encourage you to communicate how you really feel; or at least, how the comedian that you are pretending to be really feels – no one is suggesting that you should get that hot under the collar about everyday items. It's comedy, not therapy!

Be concise

Get to the point! Quickly!

The memories of every English class you ever sat through won't help you in comedy (although, later on in your career they might be a great source for parody); what you need to do is *learn to write like you speak*. Often in conversation we communicate our message without using full sentences. Normal speech jerks around all over the place. The mind leaps from place to place without worrying too much about the correct verb or even tense. So say your jokes out loud after you've written them. Can you spot any phrases that get in the way of what you are trying to say? If so, take them out.

Let's look at a couple examples of not being concise. One is extreme. The other illustrates a common mistake.

Example 1: How deadwood phrases can bury the gag

Let's return to the simplest joke in the world:

'A man walks into a bar. He hurts his head. It's an iron bar.'

Whatever your feelings on the quality of the joke, you can't deny that it is as concise as it can possibly be. There are no extra phrases that could create ambiguity in what the author is trying to say; the message is clear. Now compare that with a non-concise version of the same joke:

'This man was making his way down the street, enjoying the day, not really expecting anything untoward to happen to him, or for that matter, anything good. Then he decided to propel himself into a bar. He found the sensations he shortly experienced to be most unsatisfactory. In point of fact, to be specific, he began to experience a sharp pain around the cranial area. The silly fool had confused his categories of things completely. You see, instead of walking into a public bar – a hostelry, if you will – he had inadvertently walked into an altogether different type of bar. For this particular bar was made of iron. No wonder the poor fellow hurt his head!'

This version might work as a parody piece, but it is not a good way to communicate the comedian's message to his or her audience. The last thing you want an audience to do is to get to the end of the thought before you do.

Example 2: What happens when you throw in an extra word?

Years ago, I taught a man called Vince who wrote a great gag that got a huge reaction from his class mates. To put it into context, Vince was a huge bear of a man, with a shaven head and stubble. On stage, he looked like he had done ten rounds against the world and lost. He cultivated the air of a man continually bewildered by life. It seemed that every joke was dredged up from some deep well of misery within him. (I stress that this was the comic persona he cultivated. He was a lovely guy.) He worked in catering and was talking about hygiene in London. On the subject of vermin he had this to say:

'There are three types of rat in London:

There is the *Rattus Rattus* or Brown Rat, which is the most common.

The second type is the *Rattus Norvegicus* or Black Rat, which is responsible for the Black Death.

Then there's women.'

This unexpected 'rug pull' in the joke had the audience on the floor. It worked well for Vince because he was portraying a comic loser. Had a higher status male comic told that gag they would have come across as a lazy misogynist. With Vince, you felt he'd earned the air miles to tell that joke.

Whatever happened at his first performance, we were all sure that this joke would go down well.

On the night, I was waiting in the wings, straining to hear how the audience would react to this part. Vince seemed a bit nervous (as we all are, the first time) and this caused him to slow down ever so fractionally, as if he were a cautious driver exploring a new town. This caused him to re-write the joke on stage like this:

'There are three types of rat in London:

There is the *Rattus Rattus* or Brown Rat, which is the most common. That's the first type.

Then there is the second type of rat which is called the *Rattus Norvegicus* or Black Rat, which is responsible for the Black Death.

Then there is the third type of rat which I call women.'

The audience stared back at him, politely confused, waiting for the next bit.

It was the same thought as before, but now it sounded like, at best, a linking device to some material about ex-partners. The rhythm had changed. He had lost the juxtaposition of ideas; that mental shock of switching gears that his first version had provided now seemed a bit blurred. On that particular performance, Vince had managed to bury the gag with extra words.

So, be concise!

The longer the set up, the funnier the punchline had better be!

Think of jokes as mental 'itches' that need to be scratched. The release comes with the explosion of laughter on the punchline.

The audience are investing all of their attention in your joke and they want to be rewarded with a laugh. If the jokes are coming thick and fast, the material doesn't have to be the most profound in the world. As long as they are rewarded with a laugh, the comedian is doing their job. If, however, the comedian strings out a long 'shaggy-dog' type story, building up the audience's sense of expectation only to let it dribble away to nothing, then they are going to feel cheated.

Every well told story, whether it is humorous or not, relies on building a certain amount of tension between the teller and the listener; we all want to know what happens next. If the tension is not released at the end, we feel cross that someone has wasted our time. We need resolution. In comedy, that comes from laughing.

Obviously, this isn't to infer that a comedian should never tell long stories. Think of Ronnie Corbett's monologues when he sat in his chair on *The Two Ronnies*. He would essentially tell one long story that was peppered with funny asides, editorializing thoughts, afterthoughts and qualifications. Often as not, it was these afterthoughts that supplied the laughs, offering the audience little 'stations' along their journey. Each time Corbett got a laugh he was metaphorically scratching that laughter itch and at the same time letting the audience know they could trust him in continuing his monologue.

If an individual joke seems too long before it gets to the punchline, perhaps it would be worthwhile in going over it with a fine-tooth comb. Is every word necessary for telling the story? Are there any redundant phrases? Is there any repetition clogging up the works? If there are any words that get in the way of what is trying to be said, they should be ditched.

If it doesn't add, it detracts

We have seen how extra, empty phrases detract from the meat of your message. The audience won't laugh at your punchline if their journey to that point has become 'saggy' with extra content taking us nowhere. Similarly, there is no point in delivering a killer punchline and then drivelling on a bit more to no effect and *then* finishing the routine. A punchline, perforce, should go at the end of a joke. That's the hammer blow, after all.

Detracting the audience verbally

If you casually mention a subject then move on to something else, without addressing the first subject, then you are adding nothing to your material. For example: 'Have we got any couples in the audience, ladies and gentlemen? Really? That's nice. So, has anyone in tonight been abroad...?'. You are detracting from the momentum of your set.

The American comedy writer Gene Perret makes the point that comics are wasting time when they say things like: 'How are we all doing tonight?' He advises them to stop trying the audience's patience and get on with their jokes. You might view that as a little extreme; after all, sometimes as a comic you need to address the situation. Perhaps some trouble kicked-off in the audience just before you were introduced or you need (for whatever reason) to remind the audience that they *are* an audience. But Perret's instinct is correct. Get to the point! Don't waffle! Don't detract from what you want to say.

What are you trying to tell the audience? Is anything getting in the way of that?

Sometimes, less is more.

Detracting the audience with your body language

If you fidget unconsciously, that adds nothing to your stagecraft. Try to remember that if you are not in control of your body, then *it is in charge of you*. Do you shuffle or rock? Do you unconsciously touch your head or bring your shoulders up to protect yourself? If you do, then it may be distracting the audience from what you are trying to tell them. Are you looking down when delivering your punchlines? Then you are not letting the audience see the thoughts pass across your face. As a comic, any extraneous movement should be handled with peril.

Rowan Atkinson once said in a sketch as a French mime: 'Mah body is mah tool.' It got a huge laugh, but he is right. The only instrument you have to convey your message to an audience is your body and, by extension, your voice. Are they doing what you want them to do?

There is a great British comedian, Ian Cognito, who is one of the funniest, angriest, most energized performers you are ever likely to see. He deservedly has a bit of a cult status and a reputation for grabbing the audience by the throat and not letting go. His whole stage presence signifies that he is in charge. But conveying this to an audience is something that he had to learn.

I saw him years ago at the London Comedy Store doing an open spot at the late show – a tough gig. The first time I was booked to do a slot there, the whole of the first half (featuring three comics and a compère) was over in 15 minutes. On this particular night, Ian's material was good and the audience were lapping it up. He was fast, aggressive and witty. In anyone's eyes, it was a good performance.

A few months later I was on the same bill as him and he literally stole the show *with more or less the same material*. It was as if he had made a quantum leap in controlling the audience. I'm sure this was down to a number of factors: more gigs under his belt; polishing up his material; becoming a more confident performer. But one thing that I thought was different on that second night was his posture. At the Comedy Store, he had leaned into the audience on the balls of his feet, occasionally with his arms out as if he were trying to draw them in. It seemed to me, despite all the angry things he was saying, that the message his body was giving out to the audience was one of seeking approval. He was non-verbally asking them to like him.

At the second gig all of his weight was on the heels. He was leaning back and giving off the non-verbal message that the audience had to come to him. He had upped his status, he was now 'top dog'. In my opinion that little change in his posture changed him from subliminally saying 'like me' into saying 'I don't care if you like me, listen to me!'

Simply put, his first posture added nothing to his performance; in fact it created a dissonance.

Top tip

Don't tell us – show us

- Inhabit your stories.
- Draw the audience in.
- Look at them!

If you were telling an anecdote to a group of friends you wouldn't stare over their heads, take a deep breath and launch your soliloquy; you would make eye contact, engage them, constantly mentally 'check in' on them. Similarly, the comedian should not be 'talking at' a bunch of strangers, but rather 'talking to' a group of possible friends. The things you tell an audience are not buried in the past, they are being shared *right here and now*.

Avoid the temptation of burying your routines in the past

All this does is distance yourself from the material and your audience. As an example: psychologically you are not saying to an audience 'I was in a long term relationship that recently failed'; you are saying 'Who's been dumped recently? I have!' So remember to place everything here and now.

The comedian is not just delivering words from a page. In fact your jokes, baldly told, won't save you, but your performance *will*. So show us your thoughts. Let the audience understand what is going on in your mind.

Don't be frightened of verbally shorthanding it like you would in real life. You are not writing an essay to seek someone else's approval; you are trying to amuse people.

Top tip

Play the moment

React to what happens around you. If a police siren goes by outside, refer to it; if a squabble starts on a table, react to it; if somebody heckles you, deal with it. There is nothing worse than watching an inflexible performer not being able to go 'off script'. Most people can improvize their way through life, no one is handed an annotated script at the start of every day, telling them what to do – so why are we so scared of going into unmarked territory when on stage?

Always remember: start with your best stuff; finish with your best stuff; let the middle take care of itself

Although I run the risk of sounding like some tired old showbiz hack, it seems to me that most successful comedy shows and performances start with a bang and finish with a bang.

Some people might argue that the slow non-event of Samuel Beckett's *Waiting for Godot* is the funniest thing they've ever seen; my counter argument would be that they've never had to do 20 minutes at the Tunnel Club or the Belfast Empire.

A stand-up only has a limited amount of time to impress, especially when they are starting out and their time is restricted to a mere five minutes as an open spot act. This would not be the best time in your career to try being meditative or slow burning.

In the best of all possible worlds, all of the comedian's material should be fantastic. But for most of us, when we start out, some will be weaker than the rest. Or perhaps it's a great routine, it's just not very accessible at the beginning of your set (perhaps it's a bit dark, or mildly psychotic) and you need to build up some credit in the bank before you can unleash this particular material on an audience. For whatever reason, the comedian should always think about *starting strong and finishing strong*.

The consequences of not following this formula can be dire.

If a comic starts with weaker stuff, they are not really doing themselves any favours. They run the risk of digging a small hole from which they have to escape. An argument that newer comedians sometimes make is that they are preparing the ground for the good stuff; perhaps they feel they have to set it in context. It is a luxury that they don't really have. Also, the audience aren't going to be bowled over by the comedian's fantastic sense of structure, they – the paying punters – aren't looking for structure, they just want to laugh. Once you've proved that you can do that, you can go off in whatever direction you want (as long as they are still laughing).

Similarly, the dangers of bulking out the beginning and middle of your set with the strongest bits and then hoping to wing the rest with charm is a perilous path. If the first four minutes are funny and the last minute is so-so, I guarantee you that the audience will forget all the laughs and just feel slightly cheated.

The comedian should always start with their best material so that they can really hit the ground running; hitting the audience with their best three or four gags proves to everybody that they have a perfect right to be on stage. The audience will feel reassured, especially if the comic has been introduced as a 'new act' and therefore possibly rubbish. A strong start will buy a new comedian a little bit of breathing space. Think of it like a plane taking off; those first few jokes help the comedian attain cruising altitude, so now they can take they foot off the pedal (slightly) and enjoy the scenery.

It's most important to finish with strong material too so that you go out with a bang.

It's not a very proud admission, but we have all, at some point in our careers, rescued a lacklustre set by pulling out a great show stopping routine at the end of it all. The audience go away feeling great, but we know, in our heart of hearts, that on that particular night we have only *just* got away with it.

It is probably not good practice to get into the habit of topping and tailing your routine with your best stuff and then just meandering through the middle. This approach will never make you a great comic. The best thing a new comic could do, ultimately, is not to learn to rely on a killer opening or a strong ending, but to return to the material in the middle and see what can possibly be done to make that bit shine as brightly as the rest.

04

what sort of comic are you?

In this chapter you will learn:
- how to use flaws in your personality for comic purposes
- some essential comedy archetypes
- how to uncover what kind of comic you really are.

We have seen how playing with attitudes can unlock the humour in a subject. You can play multiple and conflicting attitudes over the course of one performance just as you would during an evening out with friends; no one would expect you to play only one note in any conversation, would they? If you did, you might find your social engagements dropping off.

Sometimes new comics find a particular attitude so liberating that they learn to present this 'face' to their audience to the exclusion of all others. Thus a deadpan depressive is born, or a hate comic. Comedians begin to develop a distinct 'persona', separate from their everyday self.

Your persona

The term 'persona' is a tricky one. Too often it can be used as a way of limiting the comedian. If they can define their comic persona within certain parameters, then they won't necessarily take risks in stepping outside that role. It may be alright for an actor to say 'my character would never do that', but it could be limiting for a comedian. Although, it would be wonderful if you could tell the audience that 'My character doesn't deal well with hecklers' or 'My character expects a standing ovation at the end.' It is not that easy to earn our spurs, I'm afraid.

Persona means the public face you present to the world. It was adopted by actors and trickled down into other performance arts, including comedy.

We all try to pigeonhole everyone, including ourselves. We have such a strong sense of self. We carry around with us a very definite sense of who we are, even if we are completely wrong about our capabilities and strengths. You may say 'I'm open-minded', but are you? Always? Have you no limits? What if we were to catch you on an off day? We all have an extremely high opinion of ourselves, but we can't *all* be right: the people who tell us (and believe) that they have a 'bubbly' personality are probably a bit dull. Similarly, it would probably be very tedious to be stuck in a lift with the 'office joker'.

This public persona that we exhibit to the world often traps us. It limits our flexibility of response, which is fatal for the comedian who should always practise being open and fluid to situations on stage, rather that fixed and rigid. The confining persona is another form of the social controller trying to dominate our lives. As long as you can don and remove these little personas that you play with, you are in control. As soon as you mistake the mask for all of you, you lose control.

Comedic flaws and how to use them

Comedic flaws are halfway between playing an attitude and developing a persona.

During a set you may play the attitudes of love, hate, worry or contempt in the course of five minutes. But those attitudes will play out differently if you have revealed the underlying character flaw of being a slob rather than being a little bit anally retentive.

Comedic flaws: Bob Hope

One of the flaws that fuelled Bob Hope's comedy was the idea that he was a complete physical coward. This in no way limited his performances in film, radio and TV. His cowardice would simply *inform* his performance. He could woo a woman (play the attitude of love), pick a fight (argumentative) or enact a business transaction (attitude of shrewdness) and at the same time leave the audience in no doubt that he was a complete chicken.

Comedic flaws: Frankie Howerd

Frankie Howerd's comedic flaw (or one of them) was his enormous sense of personal vanity. His own inflated sense of self-belief was so at odds with his shambling body and his hangdog expression that it created an instant dissonance in the audience's mind. How could this man think for a moment that he was a devil-may-care danger to women? Yet he generated much laughter over the course of his career by portraying his shambolic version of what he thought might be debonair.

Comedic flaws: Will Smith

A contemporary example is that of the very funny British comedian, Will Smith. His comedic flaws complement each other to the extent that he could almost be mistaken for a character act. He portrays himself as terminally upper middle class, with no understanding of women. He tells the women in the audience to know their strengths: while men are good at building, ladies are better at cooking, and daintiness and prettiness; his opinions make it plain why he lives alone. He is continually being ripped-off by workmen who overcharge. He is far too nice, yet deeply suspicious of anyone or anything outside his limited background. He comes from a massively dysfunctional family. He is useless at relationships; he tells us he is neither straight nor gay, he is a third category – he is *nice*.

Your take on particular attitudes will be different depending on your underlying comedic flaw. A comic who plays the flaw of being overly anxious will talk about a relationship completely differently from someone who is playing the flaw of being overly confident.

Top tip

Try this:

Look at all the different attitudes that you enjoy playing and then try to find if they all share certain qualities: in other words, could you describe them as 'symptoms' of an underlying comedic flaw or character trait? Beware of nailing down every aspect of your persona early on in your career because this could discourage you from experimentation.

Remember, while audiences don't generally like to feel confused, you have a perfect right to go off in different directions during your time on stage. You don't have to play only one emotional note. You are allowed to contradict yourself, just like you do in real life.

Comic archetypes

One of the most common questions a comedian is asked is: 'Who are your favourite comedians?' It's a bit of a red herring. We may have personal heroes, but it seems to me that most comedians admire a *type* of comedy that may or may not be epitomized by a famous stand-up: it is generally the style of comedy that we admire, rather than an individual. This is perhaps a good thing. There is nothing worse than watching a new comedian mimicking someone more famous, yet sometimes it does happen. A few years ago when Harry Hill first appeared, there were a little rash of 'Harry Hillisms' that some new comedians tried to adopt. When Eddie Izzard first made it big, there were a number of new comics who tried to copy his style.

This conscious or unconscious mimicry is always unsuccessful and should be avoided at all costs. Why would the public want a cheap imitation of someone they already like? The comedian should always strive to uncover his or her *own* voice. That is the only way to become successful.

In terms of persona, there seem to be several 'types' that occur again and again in different times and different cultures that countless comedians are happy to adopt. One final caveat, before we begin: these descriptions are not meant to be limiting to the individual performer in any way. Most comics, fairly early on discover their most successful voice quite naturally. It is only then, after the fact, that audience members start saying things like: 'You're a natural deadpan comedian, aren't you?' or 'You're a bit of a Jack the lad on stage.' But for those among us who are unsure of who we are on stage, perhaps the following types will help clarify the way you present yourself. Think of them as directions in which to travel, rather than fixed goals. There is almost infinite variety in each archetype, and the way in which you choose to inhabit one will always be different from the way someone else would. Ultimately it is *your* individuality that counts the most.

Comic loser

The world is against them. Everyone and everything is better than them. They will always seize defeat from the jaws of victory. In the game of life, they have definitely drawn the short straw. They may exhibit great dignity, as when Oliver Hardy watches the piano crash endlessly down the hill, or they may be reduced to a quivering mass of neurosis, as when a bug-eyed Rodney Dangerfield endlessly tries to loosen his tie and bemoans 'I can't get no respect!'

The comic loser's humour comes from the fact that everything they do will fail and that the petty (largely imaginary) victories that they do have will be trumpeted out of all proportion to the actual deed.

They should radiate defeat. You can be an angry loser, a sleazy loser or a loser who is in denial. In short, a loser can play just about any attitude and talk on any subject, *as long as they remain true to their nature.* They don't just crop up on a comedy stage: the cartoon character Wile. E. Coyote, always trying and eternally failing to turn Roadrunner into lunch, is probably one of the purest portrayals of a comic loser in modern times;

Charles Dickens' ever-sunny Mr Micawber could be called a comic loser; Ricky Gervais' creation of puffed-up egotist and workplace nightmare David Brent could be viewed as a comic loser.

One of the strengths of the comic loser is that he or she doesn't present a threat to an audience. We are invited to laugh *at* rather than laugh *with* their misfortunes.

Lovable buffoon

The buffoon is the slow-thinking idiot who gets everything the wrong way round. Think of Tommy Cooper, a comedian who looked perpetually bewildered by everything, including inanimate objects. Think of the early work of Lee Evans, desperately trying to win approval of his audience, while his body and thought processes run away from him.

The buffoon makes a real virtue out of that important comic device of allowing an audience to see what is passing across the comedian's face. There can be something very funny about watching the wheels turn in a comedian's brain, especially if the audience have got there first, or if the comedian's logic takes them off in a completely different direction.

Smart arse

This is the comedian who thinks that they are cleverer than they actually are: the show off; the one who can't refrain from saying the wrong thing at the wrong time; the comic with the ready, flippant remark; the know-it-all.

In the 70s, American comedian Steve Martin played with the idea of a know-it-all, arrogant Latino lover. One of the key lines in this routine was when he was demonstrating how to compliment a girlfriend's mother: 'Ah, Mrs Smith. I can see where your daughter gets her breasts! (*slight pause*) And I can see where they are going...' Classic, smart arse material.

The American comic/character act Peewee Herman summed up the energy of the smart arse with his ten-year-old's schoolyard taunt in response to every negative comment directed to him: 'I know you are, but what am I?'

Confrontationalist

This is the sort of comic who loves (or pretends to love) confronting the audience. They grab the audience by the ears and say 'Listen to this – *this* is funny.' They don't care what the audience think. It's probably fair to say that most use anger as an engine for their creativity, whether it's the cold scorn of Pat Condell ('I believe in the right to worship whatever you want, no matter how misguided, bigoted, wrongheaded or stupid that belief is...') or the dripping contempt of Mark Steel. Talking about a British politician's criticism of Muslim women wearing the face-covering niqab he says:

> 'Why didn't [Jack] Straw mention the veil to the Saudis? Somehow it all slipped his mind, and instead of questioning their ethics he sold them arms.'

(From his column in *The Independent*, 11 October 2006)

One of the most legendary performers in modern times to harness his rage is Scottish comedian Jerry Sadowitz. Calling him a legend is not empty hyperbole; stories seem to gather around Jerry like dust bunnies around static electricity. His contempt as a comedian is wide and deep, as he used to remark:

> 'People say I hate everything. That's not true. I only hate two things: people and objects.'

He will attack anything that he thinks is stupid. Picking on the political correctness of alternative comedy, he said:

> 'I'm a non-sexist, non-racist comedian, by the way. Which is a terrible shame because I've got a brilliant joke about Tina Turner.'

Turning his attention to old people, he railed:

> 'I think all pensioners should be slaughtered at birth!'

He is, as he says, '...not a 'family' comedian. Not unless you belong to the Manson family...'

In the best of all possible worlds we would have enough sensitivity not to laugh at another's pain. But since we do, Sadowitz feels that we have no right in engaging in a self-censorship that is dictated by perceived 'good taste'. What is that, after all? Is it just a collective decision? Some cultures think it is the height of good manners to have granny's bones on show above the mantelpiece. Like all good comedians, he will question your assumptions. His preferred route is through confrontation.

Genial, all round nice person

This is the type that most comedians tend to adopt, at least initially. This comedian is likable, affable and eager to engage with the audience. Their strength comes from the fact that they want to be good communicators. In talking about the world around them, they become the conduit for the audience. They become the witness, as if they were saying: 'Look, these weird things have happened to me you probably recognize them as well.' Rather than confront, they seduce an audience into their point of view. They are great charmers. Often, by plighting their craft, they find that they can lead an audience down some very disturbing paths, simply by having been nice and friendly at the beginning and building enough confidence in them as performers.

Think of it as a default stage energy for the comedian. Even at his most irate, Sadowitz would generally remember to occasionally smile and let the audience into his world.

Deadpan

If you have ever teased a friend by answering solemnly, when asked if they look like they have put on weight, 'Yes, loads', then congratulate yourself. You have deadpanned someone.

A good deadpan is hard to find. They are often the monotone, vaguely sociopathic figures who must *never* crack a smile for fear of breaking the illusion. Rather than a personality type, the deadpan delivery can just be a means to deliver the joke, pure and simple, to the audience's ear, without any sense of who the comedian actually *is* getting in the way of the joke. That is why it can be quite popular with wordsmith comics. Think of the American comedian Steven Wright. Or the 90s comedienne Hattie Hayridge, who would deliver her jokes like pebbles dropped down a well to great effect. The British comic Milton Jones crafts his jokes very carefully and, whilst not strictly speaking a deadpan, he knows the value of letting a joke stand up on its own two feet with minimal delivery:

'I was watching TV the other day and I flipped. Suddenly all I could see were my sofa cushions really close up.'

Or:

'I believe the police should be given special powers. Like flying. And turning into insects.'

These jokes would not be helped by an animated delivery.

It is arguable whether the deadpan is a proper archetypal persona: you could, after all, have comic loser deadpans or surrealist deadpans. It is, in effect, a style that most comedians dip into. Some will try it occasionally; some adopt it as their main approach.

The comic messiah

This is the comedian in tub-thumping mode. This is when, mid-rant, the stand-up transcends the role of rabble-rouser to become Moses descending from the mountain with the holy writ. It is the comic touched by greatness.

I suppose that most of us, by the ends of our sets, when we hope to have the audience in the palm of our hands, aspire to the role of comedy messiah – that glorious condition when the audience are so behind you that you can do no wrong, Some comedians, however, try to assume this archetype more completely. Think of the work of the American comedian George Carlin, who sets himself up as judge and jury of all that is wrong in western life. (If nothing else, try to listen to his anti-golf course rant, where he extrapolates, slowly but surely, with the audience cheering him all the way, that golf is a racist activity.)

The comic messiah doesn't have to make sense. In fact, it is probably best if they don't take themselves too seriously or else the magic might fly away. They just have to convince an audience for a few brief moments that they know what's what and where to put it.

The outsider

The outsider is a very powerful energy to play as a comic. It is the person looking in on society from the outside and asking why we do this or that particular thing. It can be a very effective way to point out that the emperor's new clothes are illusory. The outsider draws attention to our foibles and puts them under scrutiny.

Anyone who is foreign has the perfect right to don this persona and start asking 'Why do you people do this?' This may be the reason why many US comedians, appearing in London for the first time, bang on about pound coins, or the 'hilarious' difference between 'our words and your words' (apparently a 'fag' means something completely different in the US). Or the 'Mind the gap' messages on the Tube. The best of these, to my mind, is by comic Chris Mousicos who just shrugs and says: 'You know what? I don't mind the gap. I quite like it.'

To be able to look in, as an outsider, is a powerful weapon in the stand-up's arsenal. It is not just open to foreigners: women can use it when trying to 'explain' male behaviour; men can do it when trying to understand the opposite sex; gay comics can employ it when trying to understand what the heterosexual majority get up to.

This particular mask slips into place whenever someone asks the question 'Why do we do this?' and then tries to be objective with their answer.

The outsider, in a more extreme form, might sometimes flirt with surrealism. This leaves the audience in no doubt that their observations are well and truly off the map. We are in uncharted territory; *terra incognita*. Please hang up your assumptions at the door. Andrew Bailey, in his 25-year career, successfully bewildered and amazed audiences from a place far beyond language. He is more like a force of chaos than a human being. Early on in his career he had great success with 'Podomofski', the great Lithuanian clown who couldn't speak a word of English, but who was vaguely threatening with his bag of plastic toys. Then he re-invented himself as 'Frederick Benson', a ghoulish figure with impossibly wide shoulders who would shout bass profundo threats at the audience and march into the crowd to 'clamp' anyone who dared heckle him. He also does a mean impression of Lenin spouting nonsense. More recently, I have seen him crushed beneath a sagging eight-feet-high inflatable gorilla while he tried to carry on with his strangely musical tape loops.

On paper it sounds pointless and contrived; seen 'live' it's like watching a one-man Theatre of the Absurd. Bailey breaks every rule of set up and punchline (or rather he avoids them). The everyday world bores him. He would rather invite you into his own personal world and make you learn a new set of rules. He is, perhaps, an extreme version of the outsider.

Mixing and matching

A comedian rarely exclusively wears only one of these masks or personas detailed above, in the same way that a painter wouldn't often paint a canvas in just one colour – it might be a bit too much. Some stand-ups do embrace one archetype almost entirely, as we have seen. But the new comic should never think 'Oh, I'm obviously a comic loser' and then consciously suppress any ideas that fall outside of this area. In fact, to risk stretching the previous simile to breaking point, perhaps you should think of these personas as colours on a palate to dabble with, rather than moulds to pour yourself into.

Adopting a persona should be a way of communicating your message to the public. It shouldn't be a millstone around your neck, stifling you. At the end of the day, we are concerned with uncovering the sort of comedian you are. This is done, most simply, through the act of writing material and seeing what works and what an audience will allow you to get away with. In other words, do they buy it? If they do, then most of your worries about who you actually are as a comedian will fall by the wayside. You will *know*.

Games to uncover comedic flaws

List your comedic flaws in words and pictures

Write a list of your perceived faults and then detail how they would impact on different, specific occasions. Or if you prefer, draw a caricature or diagram of your shortcomings. Don't just focus on the negative. Try to think of ways where these flaws might be viewed as strengths: your bad anger management might mean that you always get to the front of the queue quicker!

The important thing is to remember that it is only a game! Don't start feeling you are a terrible person afterwards – it's only an aspect of yourself (and who's to say it's a real one?) that you are drawing attention to.

Exploring the flaws

Write down some character flaws that you have noticed in other people. Then exaggerate them as much as you can (for example, someone who might always like to have the last word might be shown as someone who jams their fingers in their ears and shouts 'La, la, la! I can't hear you!').

Once you feel you have a list of exaggerated flaws, write down a series of attitudes. Let these attitudes be very specific: don't write 'love', for example, write 'the love I feel towards my cat' or something similar.

Then go down your list of attitudes, in turn, and write about them as if you were trying to exhibit one particular comedic flaw. Repeat, until you have covered all the flaws. With luck, you will find yourself writing one or two jokes, and at the very least you should find some worthwhile areas worth exploring further.

part

two
practical sessions

05

unlocking your creativity

In this chapter you will learn:
- how to get yourself in the right frame of mind to write comedy
- how games can help you to create jokes
- how all creativity comes out of play.

Often, when I'm working with a group of newer comedians I will hear the complaint that they can't think of anything to say or that they feel really uncreative. What they usually mean by this is that they have plenty of ideas, but are editing them before they are even thought through because they are frightened of seeming too weird or (worse!) too banal. Sometimes, they edit themselves out of the game because they assume it's not what they think the teacher wants to hear. Whatever the reason, they are allowing that demon of social control to gain the upper hand again.

We have to trick ourselves into being creative. We have forgotten that a lot of good ideas come out of play and feel that we must be cheating someone if all our ideas aren't the product of '99% perspiration, 1% inspiration'. Blame the Protestant work ethic, blame poor teaching at a formative age, but most of us have to 'unlearn' the idea that coming up with ideas is hard. It shouldn't be. It *should* be pleasurable.

Don't worry about the result: just write!

One good way to turn that internal editor off is to allow yourself not to worry about being funny; if a funny idea occurs, good. If it doesn't immediately, tell yourself not to worry because at this stage you are only unlocking your creativity. Let any 'funniness' occur naturally without you trying to crowbar old jokes into your writing. Obviously, don't kill funny ideas that bubble up naturally by saying 'I'm not supposed to be funny yet'. If a subject doesn't seem funny yet, it may well be because you have not homed in on the subject enough.

If you have been playing with the twin ideas of getting *specific* on a subject and finding out what your *attitude* to it is, then you are probably getting a feel for how funny ideas seem to generate themselves.

Play some of the following games to trick yourself into being creative and then try the written exercises to trick your brain into writing funny stuff.

Writing activities

By this time, if you have taken two major lessons in comedy to heart (those of being specific and applying an attitude to everything you write), then you are probably well on your way to setting yourself writing tasks. The ones detailed below are just suggestions for writing games to try on those days when nothing occurs. Feel free to twist them in any personal direction you wish.

Your biography

Earlier, I asked you to write a delusional, possibly psychotic, liar's biography. This time, I would like you to write down the story of your life as you remember it happening. What happened to you to get you to this point? What chain of events propelled you to be sitting or standing, wherever you are, reading this sentence?

Feel free to skip over huge swathes of your life, as long as you touch on what you think are the salient details. Remember, no one else is ever going to read it, so be as truthful and opinionated as you like. Try, if you can, to play with moods. Don't get bogged down in the depressive stuff, so that you feel that you live in a Dostoevsky novel; nor should you be so hopelessly upbeat that it reads like one of those annual Christmas letters people photocopy and send to friends and family. ('Sadly, Granny died this year, but on a plus point, we bought a new cat!') Although that's not a bad idea for an exercise (see below).

What are your own personal triumphs and tragedies? Are there any themes that come out of your autobiography? Does the writing give you any greater understanding as to how you have got to where you are right now?

It is an exercise in pure creative writing. There will probably be few or no jokes here. It isn't, after all, written for an audience – it's just for you. But it is very difficult to get writer's block on a subject to which you are so intimately acquainted – you.

Once you have the first draft down (and we are not talking *War and Peace* length, here) why not return to a specific paragraph and try to become even more specific? What other things can you uncover about yourself or some circumstance? How much detail can you recall? Returning to a particular paragraph, can you play with a slightly more extreme attitude than the first time? If so, what direction does this take you in?

Please remember, it is not an essay. No one will be marking it. It is just you writing about your life for an audience of just you. So enjoy it.

Tree and branch

This game is called 'Tree and branch' because the writer is allowed to 'branch away' as much as they like from the main subject. You are expected to be opinionated, extreme and as obsessive as you like. Feel free to lie and exaggerate the truth. Try to fill a page on the following subjects:

- The worst holiday ever
- Why everything your Mum and Dad told you is wrong
- Unsuitable presents for children
- What not to say at a job interview
- Unsuccessful ways of getting out of being mugged
- Why clowns are evil
- Scout badges that never caught on
- What really killed off the dinosaurs
- How to feng shui a room
- The least successful British explorer
- Ways to start a pub fight
- How to stalk a celebrity
- The worst TV show in the world.

Once you've warmed up with these, get in the habit of giving yourself a title to play with and try exploring the theme. Remember, the more specific the better.

Negative school report

Write a school report for someone famous. They can be dead or alive, real or fictitious. Make sure you write teacher's comments for every subject.

A round robin letter

What would a Christmas round robin letter be like if it were written by someone who was serving life in prison or trapped on a desert island or by Attila the Hun? ('Good news! The Horde and I have sacked Rome! Again!! I grazed my knee kicking down a gate and grizzled a bit, but apart from that the New Year's looking rosy!')

Love letter from a famous person

What would a love letter from a young Henry VIII sound like, knowing what we know about him now? ('Dear Catherine of Aragon, I know technically you're still my brother's wife, but I've got to be honest – I'm losing my head over you...') What if Jack the Ripper wrote one? Or Mother Theresa?

Haiku

Haiku, as I'm sure we all know, is the Japanese verse form that only contains 17 syllables of sound. (It's actually a bit more detailed than that, but for the purposes of this game, let's just stick with this definition.) There's not a lot of room to manoeuvre within a haiku. Here's one I wrote years ago:

> 'Oh dear. Just beginning
> And already I've used up
> All my sylla-'

Your job is to write some haikus trying to address specific issues. It could be something as profound as proving the existence of God:

> 'Big beardy bloke in sky
> Must exist. Proof?
> Shooting stars are his fag ash.'

It could be as trivial as writing a haiku to dump someone:

> 'Just a short note to say
> Expect a restraining order
> In the post.'

So, set yourself some specific tasks and then use the haiku to try to address them. They don't have to be funny, they just have to fit into 17 syllables and they have to feel complete.

This game forces the writer to pare their thoughts down to the absolute minimum. It is a lesson in brevity of thought.

Rubbish superheroes

Create a useless superhero. Somebody, back in the 80s used to talk about Spiderman's lesser-known contemporary, 'Spider-Plant Man'. He was not a very active superhero, but was very good at sitting in pots in dry, sunny places.

How will your superhero's ability affect their job?

Here is the result of comedian and TV presenter Ed Petrie when he tried his hand at this exercise:

Slight Drinking Problem Man – The pitch
He's not an alcoholic – he just has a slight drinking problem.

He gets a call from the Police Commissioner – there's been a raid at the bank – the robbers have taken hostages. Slight Drinking Problem Man has a couple of whiskies – you know, just to steady his nerves – and he races over in the Tipsy Mobile. The police are relieved to see him (and of course, any mention that he may be slightly over the limit to be driving is glossed over).

He's sent forward to negotiate with the robbers. As he's talking to them they can smell whisky on his breath, and they start talking amongst themselves as to whether, you know, he might have a slight drinking problem. Whilst they're distracted he takes out a small hip flask that he carries around just in case the weather's a bit nippy and he needs warming up. He's not an alcoholic. He throws whisky in their eyes and, filled with Dutch courage, glasses them with a pint glass he nicked from the pub next door. Meanwhile the hostages have managed to escape. The criminals are arrested and the film ends with everyone having a lock-in at Slight Drinking Problem Man's local.

It'll be cheap to make. We can film it in Crawley.

Ten-word stories

This is an exercise in cutting down the information you present to the audience to a bare minimum. It's a game that Huw Thomas thought up. Simply write a story that only contains ten words. They don't even have to be grammatically correct as long as the story makes sense. (As I said at the beginning of this book, we don't talk in full sentences, so why should we write in them?) The stories might end up sounding like tabloid newspaper headlines: 'Boy meets girl, meets parents, fancies mum, dad notices. Disaster!' Or they may make some sort of lateral logic: 'A gun in your pocket? No. Bang! You're pregnant, baby!')

Huw Thomas made up a very satisfying ten-word story:

'A keen train spotter, he didn't spot the three fifteen...'

These stories can be based on personal events or things happening in the news. The only hard and fast rule is that they must contain ten words, no more and no less.

Condensed classics

Cut down some classic literature to the bare minimum, so that they are literally reduced to a handful of words. Here are a few examples:

> Dante's *Inferno*: 'I'll be damned'
> *The Old Testament*: 'You're all bad!'
> *The New Testament*: 'But I forgive you.'

You don't have to stop with classical literature: films can be fair game too. The 1940s film classic *Brief Encounter* could be reduced to: 'Hello.' 'Goodbye.'

Practise how few words you need to convey the essence of the book (or whatever sort of classic you have chosen). Or, if you prefer, think how few words you need to subvert the author's intention. Does something funny occur when you think of the title? For example, *A Brief History of Time* could be condensed down to 'The beginning, the middle and the end' without really touching on what Stephen Hawking was writing about; all you've done is make fun of the title. But similarly you could take that same book and reduce the author's message down to 'I'll write anything I like, because no one will understand it anyway' and still find that you are playing the game correctly.

The shortest play in the world

What is the shortest play in the world you could write that could tell a complete story? Here are a few titles to get you going:

- The Conquest of Everest
- 80,000 Leagues under the Sea
- The Unbearable Lightness of Being
- A Tale of Two Cities
- Love Story
- Farewell, My Lovely
- Innocence and Experience
- Stalin! The Musical.

I'm sure you can think of more. It can be a one-scene play. It could be a three-act extravaganza. The only rule is that it must be as brief as it possibly can be and still make sense. It doesn't have to make 'literal' sense: if a very satisfying three or four-word gag on the title occurs, then don't let my instructions to tell a complete story stop you from writing your idea down.

Titles for autobiographies

What might be unexpected titles for other people's autobiographies? What would be the title of your autobiography? Here are a few examples, illustrating the 'gag' nature of this afterthought game:

- 'How to Win Friends and Influence People' by Adolph Hitler
- 'Knock Three Times on the Ceiling if you Want Me (my struggle with Obsessive Compulsive Disorder)' by Howard Hughes
- 'Sex, Power and a Bit of Gardening' by Alan Titchmarsh
- 'Little Book of Calm' by Radovan Karadzic

Writing in clichés

George Orwell wrote an essay in 1946 called 'Politics and the English Language', where he spoke of (among other things) the dangers of giving yourself over to cliché when writing. His point, in a nutshell, is that when we start employing clichés then we stop saying what we mean and start to let the cliché do the thinking for us. Politicians do it all the time, it is a way of speaking without ever saying anything: 'In these troubled times, when it is darkest before the dawn, we must put our nose to the grindstone and, standing shoulder to shoulder, ride out the storm rather than reap the whirlwind…' Absolutely nothing has been said.

Your task, with this game, is to say nothing using a great deal of wind. Try not to use an original thought or phrase if a meaningless cliché will do. The idea behind the exercise is that you should try to recognize these clunking phrases that inhibit thought so that you can either avoid them or poke fun at them.

What are all those redundant phrases doing in our language? Phrases like: 'At the end of the day…'; 'My point is this…'; 'Between a rock and a hard place'; 'It boggles the mind'; 'That's let the cat out of the bag'. Even modern clichés like '24/7' or 'Talk to the hand 'cos the face ain't listening' are fair game. Happy hunting.

06 a word about emotional exaggeration

In this chapter you will learn:

- why a more extreme version of you might be more appealing to an audience
- why some comedians exaggerate their performance
- why style is so much more important than substance.

If your emotional range is narrow, you can only convey to the audience a limited range of emotions but if you work on expanding this range then you can show so much more. It is no good trying to show apoplectic rage in a comedy routine if all you can demonstrate is looking mildly peeved.

Breaking the habits of a lifetime: be bigger, be broader!

Many fledgling comedians come to the job after years of working in some incredibly 'straight' buttoned-down job. They have spent most of their adult life hiding how they really feel about things and presenting a socially acceptable face to their workmates. This means that when they begin as a stand-up, they are inhibited and use the same narrow range of social behaviour on stage that they used for years in real life. But the majority of comedians, as they continue in their careers, realize that they can be a far larger personality on stage than they ever thought possible. They begin to exaggerate their responses to things on stage because they find it gets a better response from an audience.

Reasons why comics start exaggerating their emotional responses...

- They discover that it helps enhance the attitude they're trying to communicate.
- Comedians find that the crowds love it when they show an inappropriate response towards something that is inconsequential.
- They allow the way they feel towards a certain subject to border on the obsessive.
- They find that a childish reaction is a bigger hit with the audience then a more considered reaction.
- They simply wish to appear as a more extreme personality.
- Playing with emotional extremes make them into a more compelling performer (they seem to be firing on all cylinders).

Comedians, as they progress, realize that they are able to play with the extreme attitudes *on stage* that they would normally use when they are messing around with close friends. They learn to gurn, emote, shout and 'mug up' their responses.

They learn to relax and treat the audience as if they are friends and co-conspirators, rather than a group of strangers who are passing judgement on them; they learn to exaggerate their emotional responses to get a bigger reaction from the audience. It is a slow process for some people, however, and may take years to discover.

Reasons why new comedians might overlook their emotional performance...

- Many 'rookie' comics make the fundamental mistake of thinking that their time on stage is all about the jokes they have written, so that they concentrate on the words alone and not on showing us the personality that conveys these thoughts.
- Being alone on stage, feeling exposed, can be a scary business at the beginning of a career, so they decide to play safe and not 'rock the boat'.
- It seems safer and easier, initially, to present the audience the same public persona that has helped them get by for years.

The truth of the matter is that an audience enjoys watching a good comic play around on stage. Jokes *are* an important part of that experience, but they are not the whole story; in the same way that blueprints are essential for building a house, but you need far more to build a three dimensional structure that you can live in. To put it another way, the best joke in the world will die on the teller's lips if they are not delivering it. Emotional exaggeration will help communicate your message more effectively.

Comedians who come from some other performance background instinctively 'get' this and are not shy of playing with their attitudes and their emotional responses to get a better response on stage. But don't feel too jealous of them: the actor deciding to be a comic may have to unlearn a whole set of skills to look as if they are being natural and not overly theatrical.

Why comedians need to be more extreme...

Playing with these extremes is bound to stretch you

Apart from the obvious benefit that you might actually come up with some funny ideas, you may also unlock a much more powerful emotional voice than you ever knew you possessed. Jerry Sadowitz once told me that when he first came down to London working in a nine to five job, he was shocked to realize that good things didn't automatically happen to nice people. He felt a growing rage at being ignored and marginalized socially and at work. Girls didn't want to go out with him; colleagues didn't know he was there; he was considered the opposite of 'cool'. He said that when he discovered stand-up it was like a demon being unleashed: all that anger became a driving force for his comedy and an engine for his creativity. Had he not vented his spleen and given voice to these extreme emotions, had he instead chosen to continue playing the 'Mr Nice' that was getting him nowhere at work, then chances are we would never have heard of him.

It's good to play games that let you off the hook

It is enormous fun to explore the limits of what you are capable of saying or showing within the safe confines of a game. It liberates the spirit to be able to act like an extreme emotional idiot and realize that people are willing you to go further. You realize afterwards that the sky hasn't fallen, or that everyone else isn't looking away in disgust and you begin to realize how illusory and limiting your own sense of personal dignity actually is. This is a very good thing for a comedian to discover.

It's good to step outside your personal comfort zone occasionally

Once you are off the edge of your own personal psychological map, you may discover much more entertaining subjects and approaches.

You must learn to distrust your idea of who you are

It is, after all, just another way of that editing social controller inside of you trying to narrow you down. No one cares how 'sensitive' or 'responsible' you may want to appear. You are not on stage to look 'cool' or 'sexy' or 'wise' or 'sensible'.

> **Remember**
>
> You are on stage to make people laugh!
>
> A comedian is paid to be a fool, not a rock star! Our sense of dignity is not important.
>
> Unfortunately, there are no good ways to learn how to present extreme states by yourself. You need an audience present to gauge the reaction to your play. Exploring your emotional range can only come through live experience.

Activities to encourage emotional exaggeration

Here are some group games that might help if you are lucky enough to be working with like-minded people.

Fear, love, hatred and lust

The group splits into two groups. One half will be the performers, the other half will be the audience. One person will have to step outside the game to offer to lead the participants. They tell the groups that the only rules in all these four games is that performers are not allowed to pick things up (like chairs, for example), and they are not allowed to get closer to the audience than five feet. The game leader might want to draw out an invisible line that the performers are not allowed to step over.

- **Fear:** The performers line up in front of the audience and let the rest know that there is something behind the audience's back which is frightening them. They must try to communicate their fear to all the members of the audience and not just pick on the person directly before them. The performers start 'small', just exhibiting mild panic or apprehension, but every time the game leader claps their hands and shouts 'Get bigger' they ratchet up the emotional level they are conveying. Pretty soon they are so terrified that they are all beyond words, just gibbering like idiots. Each time they hear the game leader shout 'Get bigger' they become more grotesque and caricatured until finally the audience must feel they are watching some scene from Bedlam. When they can get no bigger (and remember, bigger doesn't necessarily mean louder – so don't strain your throat) the game leader shouts 'Relax' and they can all stop. He or she will then take an imaginary snapshot of absolute, abject fear after a count of three.

It is then the turn of the audience half to become the performers, while the other half sit down to watch their turn. They must try to outdo the intensity of the first group.

- **Love:** The first group stands in a line again and this time must convey (ultimately) a cloying, sentimental love that they feel towards all of the audience. Again, they should start small, so that they have somewhere to travel to, and as the game leader claps and shouts 'Get bigger' they become more and more extreme. Eventually they should be a quivering mass of undignified, raw neediness. The game leader takes one final snapshot of ultimate love, and then the groups swap and it is time for the other half to have a go.

- **Anger:** This is exactly the same, but with anger. Start with mild dislike and build to a towering, red rage towards the audience. Once you become larger than life and you feel you can travel no further, try pushing the performance out a little more; perhaps start showing them what you will do to them if you ever get your hands on them, or building up into a cartoon of pent up anger even more. Eventually each group will travel beyond words with each of these emotional states and that is where, often, the fun can begin. When they can go no further, the game leader shouts 'Relax', then takes one final snapshot for posterity. Then the other half takes their turn.

- **Lust:** This time, each group starts with mild attraction to the entire audience; the flirting soon builds to wild abandon and finally grotesque loss of control. A snapshot is again taken at the end, and then the other group can try.

Sometimes individuals can beat themselves up psychologically because they feel that they are blocking themselves and can't 'do' one emotional extreme or another. If this happens to you, just let yourself off the hook. Take heart that no one is going to ask you to do this for 20 minutes a night as a career. It's just a game.

Hitch-hikers

This is an old 'improv' game that I've seen performed all over the country. Everyone should split into groups of four. Each group will perform this game in front of the rest who act as an audience.

Set out four chairs or stools, two in the front and two behind; this will be the car for the purposes of the exercise. One person will choose to be the driver and each of the other three is given an extreme emotional state to play. They might be timid, suspicious, angry, judgemental, sarcastic, sympathetic or any other state as long as it is extreme. Get the audience to nominate states for each of the passengers; this is quite a good way for the group to ensure that individuals are pushed outside their 'comfort' zone. It might be quite fun to see someone who is good at self-deprecation being forced to play a gigantic egotist. Make sure that these suggestions are 'one-note' moods. Sometimes an audience member might suggest something ambiguous like 'psychotic', but that isn't really an emotion (you could be a happy psychotic or a sad psychotic, after all) so make sure each of the three passengers are crystal clear as to what their emotional state should be.

The driver must act out a scene, with the others, where he or she will pick up three hitch-hikers. As soon as the first passenger is picked up, both they and the driver adopt that particular emotional state (let's for the sake of argument, say 'love'). After a while the second hitch-hiker thumbs a lift and as soon as they are in the car all three of them adopt this second emotional state (let's say 'hate'). When the third passenger eventually gets in all four of them switch to the third passenger's emotional state (let's say 'fear').

After a while, the third passenger feels that they are arriving at their destination and leaves. As soon as he or she is out of the car, the rest of them revert to the second hitch-hikers emotional state (hate). Then, when the second traveller decides to get out the first passenger and the driver revert to the first passenger's emotional state (love), until eventually the first passenger gets out and the driver goes on their merry way. Game over.

To stop things getting a little sticky or formless for the first couple of games, the group could always nominate an outside director who moves things along by shouting out helpful things like 'They see a second hitch-hiker' or 'The third hitch-hiker thinks they are getting near their destination.' But after a couple of goes, everyone should have a feel for the game and be able to judge when they get in and out of the car.

Don't be daunted by the game. All the players have to do is think of the emotional states they are trying to show and to make sure that they are really listening to what the other people in the car are saying. Some of the funniest moments can come when everyone is simply reacting and not trying to take control of the scene. It's also quite satisfying for the audience to watch a carload of people turn on a sixpence from one extreme emotion to a completely different one.

Apart from playing with emotional extremes, this can also be a very reassuring exercise for those taking part: often they can experience that glorious joy of collectively creating something out of nothing.

The off

This is a great game for pairs that Huw Thomas uses. Not only does it encourage emotional exaggeration, it also helps the comedian practise the art of saying one thing while revealing another.

The pair act out a scene where they play two cowards about to have a fight. They are extremely angry towards each other and are about to knock the other one unconscious, but at the same time they are both complete moral and physical cowards. If one of them makes a sudden movement, then the other one flinches – or better still, shrieks in terror – then tries to be brave again. If the game is going well, there should be at least seven or eight feet between the protagonists. If the energy starts flagging, have one outsider nominated so that they can shout out 'Be angrier!' or 'Be more scared!' as the occasion demands. Make sure that the players really push themselves into emotional extremes.

creating material

In this chapter you will learn:
- how to mine your head for ideas
- how to turn ideas into jokes
- how to take responsibility and workshop your own ideas.

Let us get down to the business of crafting material. You may have found by this point that you have generated quite a bit of material from some of the games detailed in previous chapters. If so, well done! Book yourself a gig and try it out in front of a live crowd.

But getting results from a creativity exercise is only half the job.

What this chapter is going to attempt to do is to train you to further mine your head for funny ideas.

Lists are a great way to generate material: they give you something to aim for, rather than just letting your pen hover above the paper waiting for inspiration to strike. A list also frees us from the tyranny of feeling we have to write an essay on any subject. It means that we can write as much or as little as we want on a specific subject before moving on to the next item on our list.

Years ago, the comedian Tony Allen came up with a writing exercise where the comic had to thank a list of people who had affected his or her life. Many of his students found it beneficial in focusing their minds. But why stop with just people? Shouldn't the job of the comic be to draw attention to everything that takes his or her fancy? That is what I would like you to do for *your* version of a thank you list.

Workshop 1: The thank you list

For your first list, write down all the things in the world that you would like to thank. It is *your* list, so be as personal as you like, and get bogged down in as much minutiae as you like. If you have a secret passion for something that is deemed 'uncool', now is the time to revel in it. Trainspotting, live historical battle re-enactments or collecting 'Pokemon' cards (should they be your particular cup of tea) are all grist to the mill. It is going to be the 'first draft' of your thoughts, so don't worry about what other people might think. The only golden rule for this exercise is BE SPECIFIC. Really think about what you want to thank; don't say 'Chinese food' if what you really mean is 'Shark fin soup'.

Here are a few pointers:

• Don't worry about whether or not it will sound very interesting to your audience. It *must* be of interest to you. What you have to say about your life will be infinitely fascinating to the rest of us *if it matters to you*. So don't edit yourself.

- Do show us how you feel towards the subject (your attitude, in other words).
- Don't feel you have to be funny. (It is a first draft, after all.) If a funny idea occurs, then all well and good, but don't feel the need to crowbar 'gag' endings in just yet.
- Try to keep the ideas open-ended so that you can return to them later.
- Feel free to use an afterthought if one occurs.
- Some things may not need explanations, as far as you are concerned.
- Even though it is a fairly positive thank you list, feel free to be sarcastic, bitter, sardonic or hypocritical in your approach to individual subjects; it may, for example, sound more like a hate list, masquerading as a thank you list. You should not feel reined in by the exercise: comedians in the past have made them sound like Oscar acceptance speeches or a letter to God or a very bitter string of bullet points to ex-lovers. So, as with all the other written exercises in this book, feel free to make your own personal game out of it. If you are excited by the direction you are going in then there is a good chance that your audience will be too.

The First World War poet Rupert Brooke wrote a fantastic example of a heartfelt thank you list in his poem 'The Great Lover'. In it, he draws the reader's attention to all the things that matter to him, greedily trying to list them all before a soldier's death takes him. This may seem a strange example to give for a comedy exercise, but you could do a lot worse than emulate his attention to detail and his celebration of the mundane.

Here's the second half of the poem:

These I have loved:
White plates and cups, clean-gleaming,
Ringed with blue lines; and feathery, faery dust;
Wet roofs, beneath the lamp-light; the strong crust
Of friendly bread; and many-tasting food;
Rainbows; and the blue bitter smoke of wood;
And radiant raindrops couching in cool flowers;
And flowers themselves, that sway through sunny hours,
Dreaming of moths that drink them under the moon;
Then, the cool kindliness of sheets, that soon
Smooth away trouble; and the rough male kiss
Of blankets; grainy wood; live hair that is
Shining and free; blue-massing clouds; the keen

Unpassioned beauty of a great machine;
The benison of hot water; furs to touch;
The good smell of old clothes; and other such
The comfortable smell of friendly fingers,
Hair's fragrance, and the musty reek that lingers
About dead leaves and last year's ferns...
Dear names,
And thousand other throng to me! Royal flames;
Sweet water's dimpling laugh from tap or spring;
Holes in the ground; and voices that do sing;
Voices in laughter, too; and body's pain,
Soon turned to peace; and the deep-panting train;
Firm sands; the little dulling edge of foam
That browns and dwindles as the wave goes home;
And washen stones, gay for an hour; the cold
Graveness of iron; moist black earthen mould;
Sleep; and high places; footprints in the dew;
And oaks; and brown horse-chestnuts, glossy-new;
And new-peeled sticks; and shining pools on grass;
All these have been my loves. And these shall pass,
Whatever passes not, in the great hour,
Nor all my passion, all my prayers, have power
To hold them with me through the gate of Death.
They'll play deserter, turn with the traitor breath,
Break the high bond we made, and sell Love's trust
And sacramented covenant to the dust.
– Oh, never a doubt but, somewhere, I shall wake,
And give what's left of love again, and make
New friends, now strangers...
But the best I've known
Stays here, and changes, breaks, grows old, is blown
About the winds of the world, and fades from brains
Of living men, and dies.
Nothing remains.

O dear my loves, O faithless, once again
This one last gift I give: that after men
Shall know, and later lovers, far-removed,
Praise you, 'All these were lovely'; say 'He loved'.

Now, with huge apologies to the estate of Rupert Brooke, let us use his poem as the basis of what a sample thank you list might look like.

The first thing to be said is that each of these observations that Brooke makes matter passionately to him. He is clearly writing for himself – he is not trying to please anyone else, he has complete confidence that what he has to say will matter to us. As such it holds our attention completely, almost a hundred years after it was written. So have faith in your own observations and, like his example, make your list a detailed list.

Breaking down his poem, we might list his great loves as:

- White plates and cups, clean-gleaming, ringed with blue lines and feathery, faery dust
- Wet roofs, beneath the lamp-light
- The strong crust of friendly bread
- Food and all it's different flavours
- Rainbows
- The blue bitter smoke of wood
- Radiant raindrops couching in cool flowers
- Flowers themselves, that sway through sunny hours, dreaming of moths that drink them under the moon
- The cool kindliness of sheets, that soon smooth away trouble
- The rough male kiss of blankets
- Grainy wood
- Live hair that is shining and free
- Blue-massing clouds
- The keen unpassioned beauty of a great machine
- The benison of hot water
- Furs to touch
- The good smell of old clothes
- The comfortable smell of friendly fingers
- Hair's fragrance
- The musty reek that lingers about dead leaves and last year's ferns
- Dear names
- Royal flames
- Sweet water's dimpling laugh from tap or spring;
- Holes in the ground
- Singing voices
- Voices in laughter
- A body's pain, (soon turned to peace)
- The deep-panting train
- Firm sands
- The little dulling edge of foam that browns and dwindles as the wave goes home
- Gleaming wet washed stones, gay for an hour
- The cold graveness of iron
- Moist black earthen mould
- Sleep
- High places
- Footprints in the dew
- Oak trees
- Brown, new glossy horse-chestnuts
- New-peeled sticks
- Shining pools on grass

This is a pretty perfect list of items. He makes us think in a new way (his way!) about familiar things ('The comfortable smell of friendly fingers'); he's not shy of stating the obvious ('Aren't rainbows great?'); he even supplies his own afterthoughts on occasion ('...and body's pain, soon turned to peace;') We can see how, sometimes, one thought will lead to another – from sand beaches his mind goes on to sea foam. Sometimes he explains why he takes pleasure in a thing ('...the cool kindliness of sheets, that soon smooth away trouble;') and sometimes he feels he needn't bother ('grainy wood').

Write your thank you list with the same sense of passion and commitment that Rupert Brooke did. Feel free to go into much greater detail than he did and feel free to add any afterthoughts as they occur. Don't worry about being funny just yet, but do make sure that you *are* specific. Being specific leads to material!

Workshop 2: Building routines

Once you have written your list and you are sure that everything on the list is something you feel strongly about and want to share with the audience, then return to the list and start adding opinionated or flippant afterthoughts. Be prepared to undercut your initial statement with something that is selfish, mildly sociopathic or just shows that you have got completely the wrong end of the stick. In other words, try to surprise and confound your audience with the second half of the statement. Feel free to add afterthought to afterthoughts, rather like in the 'When I say that, what I really mean is...' exercise in Chapter 02.

Break it down!

One way to do this is to break each of your statements down into smaller chunks of information. For instance, the sentence 'I like nothing better on a Sunday morning than to read a selection of newspapers in bed with my lover over a cup of tea' contains the following pieces of information:

'I like nothing better on a Sunday morning
than to read a selection of newspapers
in bed
with my lover
over a cup of tea.'

If we were to add a flippant afterthought or stupid editorializing point to each of these statements we might find that we now have:

- 'I like nothing better on a Sunday morning (and it must be a Sunday morning – try doing it on a Tuesday afternoon and you'll only get into trouble at work)
- than to read a selection of newspapers (well, I say 'read' – some of the words are a bit long – but I can usually work out what's happening if there is a picture)
- in bed (it's not as relaxing lying on a table)
- with my lover (although I've got to be careful – I think my wife is beginning to suspect)
- over a cup of tea.' (literally suspended over a cup of tea – it's an old tantric trick I picked up in the East – it really opens up the pores)

Once more – with feeling!

We could even start adding afterthoughts to afterthoughts. For example, what is the comedian's definition of 'quality' newspapers? Perhaps they read *The News of the World* (for political commentary, obviously) or perhaps they avoid the *Mail on Sunday*, finding it too liberal ('Not enough articles about immigrants coming over here and stealing our jobs!'). Perhaps for pleasure they turn to the 'North Yorkshire Pig Breeders Gazette'.

Clearly, at this stage we are in danger of overwriting the original statement into the ground. But this shouldn't worry us too much just yet, as we can always cut the bits not going anywhere later on. At this stage, it is the exploration of the thought that matters the most. As long as we get one or two funny afterthoughts out of the exercise then it will be worthwhile.

Adding afterthought to your thank you list

Let us now return to Rupert Brooke's poem and perform an unforgivable literary crime by attempting to 'gag up' the first few lines of 'The Great Lover'. The afterthoughts are placed in brackets.

White plates and cups... (although patterned plates and cups are better, then you don't have to worry about giving them too thorough a washing up – better still, if you have a pet dog, let them lick the plates clean as they are very good at it and it'll save you more time for other domestic tasks like spying on your neighbours or watching TV)

Wet roofs, beneath the lamp-light (because they always remind me how happy I am to live in such a wet, dark, miserable country)

The strong crust of friendly bread (but avoid the strong crust of rice pudding – it's a sure sign of salmonella...)

Food and all it's different flavours (in the case of British Cuisine this basically means either 'salty' or 'mushy' – usually both...)

Rainbows (as opposed to the children's lunchtime show *Rainbow*, which corrupted a nation's youth by showing Zippy and Bungle sharing a bed. They weren't even the same species!)

The blue bitter smoke of wood (although be careful, it could mean your shed is on fire...)

Radiant raindrops couching in cool flowers (if you've never seen a 'radiant raindrop', try watching the clouds above Chernobyl. They glow in the dark)

Flowers themselves, that sway through sunny hours, dreaming of moths that drink them under the moon (sorry, I'm having an LSD flashback...)

The rough male kiss of blankets (rough male kisses are pretty cool, too – if you don't mind stubble rash...)

Grainy wood (got to get your roughage from somewhere, after all...)

Live hair that is shining and free (not like toupees, which cost far too much and always look unconvincing)

Blue-massing clouds (are best avoided during hurricane season – it could get a bit 'blowy'. Look at New Orleans)

The keen unpassioned beauty of a great machine (I mean – I only like them, I'm not a freak or anything. I once went out with a toaster, but she left me. Commitment issues. And her warranty ran out...)

The benison of hot water (is always great unless you're a hydrophobe)

Furs to touch (but please make sure the animal is sedated before you try this one out at home, kids...)

The good smell of old clothes (although this doesn't explain why charity shops reek of despair and soup)

The comfortable smell of friendly fingers (don't make a nuisance of yourself going around sniffing fingers, however – it's not really a solid basis for friendships)

Hair's fragrance (especially if the hair owner is familiar with the concept of washing it. Otherwise, stand up wind of them and, if you must, concentrate on sniffing their fingers)

The musty reek that lingers about dead leaves and last year's ferns (very handy, as it can help mask the smell of the bodies you've buried)

Feel free to carry on this game, adding your own afterthoughts to Brooke's list.

But the most important thing for you to do is to get working at refining your own thank you list.

Be flippant, be opinionated and be stupid with those afterthoughts.

Chances are, if you have changed each item on your original list to a thought and then a surprising afterthought, you will probably have written the beginnings of a joke.

Workshop 3: Putting your set together

Use all the tricks you've learnt thus far on a second draft thank you list. Be prepared to explore every aspect of the subject, turning off on as many side roads as you like.

Push your attitudes to bigger extremes; explore the gap between a high aspiration and a low reality. Be prepared to go off on a tangent and, if necessary, dump the original thought and concentrate on pursuing the afterthought to an illogical, extreme conclusion.

Top tip

- Don't put all the same types of jokes together – audiences want to be surprised, they certainly don't want to start guessing the mechanisms you are using to make them laugh.
- Top and tail your set with your best stuff, so you hit the ground running and leave them wanting more.
- Remember to write how you speak; your material must sound natural to you.
- Always work on your weakest bits. Why are some parts weaker than others? Are you being specific enough? Are you pushing an extreme attitude enough? Is your afterthought too vague? Should you be exaggerating your emotional responses more?

Opening out your ideas

Let us return to Rupert Brooke's thank you list to demonstrate how we might refine our own list. Let's take the very first item and see how we can open it up further. I've put explanations of what we are doing with the text in bracketed capitals.

White plates and cups

Aren't white plates and cups a bugger to clean? (THOUGHT)

I think we should all use paper ones – sod the environment – what have trees ever done for us? (ATTITUDE AND AFTERTHOUGHT)

Sucking up all that carbon dioxide and pumping out oxygen and interfering with global warming. (AFTERTHOUGHT TO AN AFTERTHOUGHT)

I happen to *like* hot summers, as it happens. (AFTERTHOUGHT TO AN AFTERTHOUGHT)

I hate it when you go round to someone's dinner party... (CHANGE OF SUBJECT)

...and they make you feel all uptight by getting their best china out... (OPINIONATED ATTITUDE)

...that's going to go down well with the six pack of Special Brew you've brought along. (AFTERTHOUGHT)

My general rule of thumb is the better the plates... (THOUGHT)

...the less chance of copping off with an emotionally vulnerable woman in the downstairs loo. (AFTERTHOUGHT)

I mean, that's what we all want from a party, isn't it? The chance of illicit sex and a massive hangover – not nice plates and Pan-Pacific cuisine. (QUALIFYING AFTERTHOUGHTS)

Also, you can't relax if you're eating off plates that cost more than your last car. (EXAGGERATION)

Middle class people can't just brag about it, though, they have to find subtle ways of letting you know just how loaded they are:

'Do you like our crockery? We picked it up from a delightful market stall in Bali. Have you been? Oh, you MUST! These plates are all individually handcrafted with religious motifs by the chap's family – apparently he can't afford to send them to school – and I suppose it's much better that they learn a trade. They only cost us 48 rupai EACH! Which works out at about ten pence a plate – so we both thought 'What the hell? How many times are we in a Third World country?' The man wanted ten pence each – but we beat him down to seven – honestly, they do try to rip you off. So, all in all, they were quite a bargain. Admittedly, it cost us 140 pounds to ship them back, but still they're a bargain!' (CARTOONING OUT A SCENE AS AN EXTREME CHARACTER)

A couple of tips if you are having a dinner party:

Number one: Don't. (ATTITUDE)

Number two: If you *must* invite people round, always use patterned plates... (THOUGHT)

...then you don't have to worry about giving them too thorough a washing-up before the do. (AFTERTHOUGHT)

Better still, if you have a pet dog, let them lick the plates clean as they are very good at it. (AFTERTHOUGHT TO AN AFTERTHOUGHT)

If you haven't got a dog, get an old person to do it. (ANOTHER AFTERTHOUGHT)

They love a hot meal. (AFTERTHOUGHT TO AN AFTERTHOUGHT)

Or at least, the remains of a hot meal. (AFTERTHOUGHT TO AN AFTERTHOUGHT)

It'll save you more time for other domestic tasks... (THOUGHT)

...like spying on your neighbours or watching TV. (AFTERTHOUGHT)

Pruning your material

Once the material is fully explored and you feel you are beginning to like its shape, be prepared to cut out any deadwood. What words or phrases are redundant? What bits hinder the story that you are trying to tell? Take them out!

This may feel counter-intuitive after all the talk throughout this book of not editing your thoughts, but at some point we have to start taking control of our material. As a general rule of thumb, we should start the editing process only once the creative process is finished.

'Less is more' activities

The 'Ten word story game' in Chapter 05 is a good game to encourage your editing skills, as is the 'Shortest play in the world game'. Here are a couple of other editing exercises that encourage clarity of thought.

Haiku 'break up' letters from famous lovers

See the earlier haiku challenge on page 69. This time, dump someone in only 17 syllables. Imagine famous lovers from history. What would their haikus be like?

Classical texting

Reduce a well-known classical story to a text message; the shorter, the better. For instance 'Oedipus' could be 'Mum! U look Gr8! O no! I've gone blind!'

Newspaper headlines dialogue

Write a simple everyday scene set in some mundane place like a doctor's office or a restaurant. Be as humdrum as you like. Then re-write the dialogue as if you were a coffee-fuelled tabloid newspaper subeditor. Pare every statement down to its barest minimum. For example, the sentence, 'I'm afraid the test results don't look very encouraging, Mr Whinstanley', might become 'Doc's shock rocks patient's world!'

Workshop 4: The hate list

This workshop is attempting to throw you into much deeper waters than the thank you list, if for no other reason than you should attempt to apply all the lessons learnt in the previous workshops when working on this particular list. So, at the very least, try to make your first draft include afterthoughts from the beginning.

Remember to include extreme attitudes and emotionally exaggerate your responses to the various subjects raised.

Follow these steps:

1 Write a hate list of all the things and people that irritate you. Remember to be specific.
2 Redraft it, cutting out any deadwood and refining any afterthoughts to become even more extreme or surprising.
3 Order the thoughts so that material is topped and tailed by your best stuff or so that hate subjects around the same area are grouped together to become mini routines. For example, you may want to put all your thoughts on young people behaving badly in public, your childhood, school days and fashion mistakes you've made in the past under one unspoken subheading of 'What I hate about being young'. Similarly, you could take hate lines about getting up in the morning, bad breakfasts, public transport, taking the car on journeys and office politics and weave them all into one long routine under the unspoken title of 'How my mornings suck'. By grouping like-minded jokes together, we can begin to build up routines.
4 Take a final look at your hate list, reading it out loud to see if it sounds natural, rather than an essay, and jot down any other ideas that help make the piece funnier.

Let's leave Rupert Brooke in peace this time around, but if you wanted to, as a separate exercise in exploring extreme attitudes, you could take his list from 'The Great Lover' and re-write it as a hate list. The subjects won't be personal to you, but the explorations might be fun. I for one would probably pay good money to watch someone get incandescently angry about blankets, sheets and rainbows.

Workshop 5: Creating your own lists

Once you have gotten into the swing of things with the first two lists and you find yourself becoming increasingly specific in your explorations, you will probably find that more and more lists begin to occur to you. Feel free to explore all the side roads that are opening up before you. For example, a list detailing the crushes you suffered in childhood could easily lead on to a list of the ways you were dumped as a teen or the ways you dumped other people; this in turn could lead to a list of how to behave on a first date, or a list of warning signs of how to tell whether someone is getting too serious about you, or reasons for moving in with someone.

The list is a great mechanism for breaking down the raw material of life into smaller, more manageable chunks of experience that could yield some very funny observations. In the first workshop we had a list with the underlying flavour of 'I love it'; in our fourth workshop we played with the attitude of 'I hate it'. We could have just as easily written a worry list or a list of things that frighten us or a list of things that begin with the words 'I am jealous of...'; these particular emotional extremes would have generated afterthoughts just as fruitful as the first two lists.

Here is a list of titles that you may wish to explore while you are waiting for your own specific lists to occur:

- Things I don't understand
- Things I don't/can't/shouldn't do anymore
- Things people don't know about me
- Things I'd like to change about my friends
- Things I have lost
- What people say and what they really mean (with examples)
- Books yet to be written
- Weird things people say
- Things that prove the existence of God
- Things that disprove the existence of God
- Suitable punishments for specific crimes/celebrities
- Bad ideas
- What I thought as a child
- Things not to say or do on a first date
- What I should have said is…
- Ridiculous ad campaigns
- Oxymorons (e.g. Drink responsibly; Military intelligence)
- Family holidays are great because…
- Family holidays are intrinsically evil because…

Think laterally

Do remember that your exploration of a list doesn't have to be entirely verbal (although, it may be). Your list could include diagrams, cartoons, mind-maps or pictures ripped out of magazines. Use whatever means necessary to convey the initial thoughts out of your head and into the world.

Workshop 6: Joke forms

Obviously as a comedian you can't stand on stage for 20 minutes or more starting each sentence with 'I hate…' or 'I'd like to thank…' – that would get very dull very quickly. So let us look at some of the tricks and approaches that stand-ups use to dress up their material. It is by no means a complete list, but it does cover the most basic joke forms that comedians tend to use.

Try writing some material using these joke forms. They may not make the final cut of your set, but it will be an opportunity to exercise those bits of your brain that come up with funny ideas.

The rule of three

There is a very pleasing rhythm of speech involving bunching three things together. If you think about phrases like 'faith, hope and charity' or 'blood, sweat and tears', you'll begin to realize that, in the English language at least, there is something very satisfying about these little triads of thought. They seem, somehow, to be complete. Think of patriotic politicians who say things like 'It's the right way, it's the only way, it's the *British* way.' They have learnt that these sorts of triple thoughts are what press the buttons of their audience.

This means that the comedian has a ready-made rhythm to exploit and subvert. The speech pattern has to contain three clauses, not four – that would seem unwieldy. This may be the reason why pub jokes feature (for example) an Englishman, an Irishman and a Scotsman, rather than an Englishman, an Irishman and a Scotsman and *also a Welshman*. Paradoxically more information would make the joke structure seem less complete.

The mechanics of a rule of three gag are: Introduce, Reinforce, Subvert. That is to say:

you *introduce* the subject or example;
you *reinforce* the logic of the subject;
then you *subvert* our expectations by offering us a surprise twist.

Traditional example of the rule of three

So, for example, in the pub joke the Englishman introduces or demonstrates, the Scotsman reinforces the logic of the joke and the Irishman subverts it all by offering us a 'surprise' solution or misunderstanding.

Observational example of the rule of three

'There are some great things about being single.

You can get up when you want. (INTRODUCTION)

Never argue over the washing up. (REINFORCE)

No one asks awkward questions when you're hanging around graveyards.'(SUBVERT)

The subversion has some logic to it, but it is not an everyday logic – it is the *comedian's* logic.

Effectively, the rule of three joke is still an afterthought gag. So don't get bamboozled when other comedians are bandying the term around. All the comedian is doing is building up his or her case with two thoughts, rather than the usual one, before knocking them down with the third.

So, now that you understand it, write some 'rule of three' jokes.

The reversal gag

This is sometimes known as 'the switcheroo' or 'the reveal'. Most comedians at some point in their career will use a reversal gag. It happens when you trick the audience by switching meaning or context. They think you are taking them down one path and then you surprise them with a sudden change of direction. You *reverse* their expectations.

A typical reversal gag might run:

'My girlfriend and I decided to spice up our sex life when we saw a copy of the *Kama Sutra* in a local bookshop. And I've got to say, it was the best thing we ever did. We were getting into positions we'd never thought of before, but also it was like we reached a new level of intimacy and love. To be honest, I thought that I might achieve the first ever male multiple orgasm except that the shop owner asked us if we could stop as we were putting off his other customers.'

The joke takes the audience down one path, and then switches lanes on them.

A shorter version of the reversal gag, taken from the set of Ronnie Rigsby is:

'I like to cheer people up at funerals. I put my head against the coffin and say, "I think I can hear a noise."'

Try writing some of your own reversal gags. Inappropriate or flippant afterthoughts may help you find the reversal that you need. Sometimes the drop from high concept to low comedy can provide the solution we require to generate a laugh.

Which leads us very nicely onto the next joke form.

Big, big, small

Take a subject and go from the profound to the mundane. Start cosmic and become tedious. Brenda Gilhooley used to have a line that went something like:

> 'I'm going on hunger strike to protest about women's rights in the Third World.
>
> I'm going to support their rights for universal emancipation!
>
> I'm going to man the barricades until patriarchy comes crashing down!
>
> I'm going to fit into a size ten!'

She has comically subverted a massive political issue.

Tony Allen used to tell a really long cosmic shaggy dog story exploring the nature of the universe by beginning with the observation that we are these fleeting, fragile specks moving around on a tiny mote revolving around an insignificant star, separated by a vast, incomprehensible gulf from other insignificant stars. He would keep lifting the orders of magnitude, to portray the vast dance of the galaxies, the nature of time and the inevitably slow decay of everything, even atoms, billions and billions of years hence. His punchline was that, given all this, it doesn't really matter whether he has a good gig or not. That's a pretty profound drop, from the majesty of the heavens to a stand-up worrying about dying on stage...

So write some jokes taking us from the sublime to the ridiculous.

The rant

This is the obsessive emotional tirade of the comic. It could be you metaphorically rolling up your sleeves to demolish a subject or it could be you standing on your soapbox preaching your point of view. A successful rant must be a sustained outburst that doesn't allow the audience a breathing space. It is often, but not always, an attack on something that the comedian disagrees with. It must be fuelled by anger – it's very hard to imagine a laid-back rant.

Of course, you don't want to degenerate into a bile-spitting comedian melting into a pile of impotent rage – you want to make sure the rant is funny.

One way of doing this is writing a first draft, bullet-pointing all the things you need to say. Then on the second draft, break each statement down and think of a stupid afterthought or qualification. Sometimes this alone can point out the poor logic of the idea that is upsetting you and, if not, then perhaps use analogy to make your point. The key point is, as always, break it down, get specific then supply the twisted afterthought.

The logical illogical conclusion of things

This is quite a useful writing trick. It is when the comic extends the logic of a particular argument to breaking point and beyond to reveal the absurdity in being too literal minded. The joke usually hinges on a misunderstanding of categories or it can be born out of a certain rigidity of thought. It may be dressed up as a 'rule of three' gag or take the form of a rant or indeed any other type of joke that we can care to think of. It may be a snappy one-liner, or it may be an opportunity for the comic to show exactly why they would make a terrible philosopher, as they carefully build up their forensic argument to reach a completely wrongheaded solution.

Here are a couple of examples:

'I hate all intolerant people; they should be shot at birth.'

A simple 'thought/afterthought' joke, playing with universal statements. As a comic, you should look for over-generalized definitive statements, like 'all cats are evil' or 'cheaters never prosper' as they are begging to have holes picked in their logic.

'Live every day like it's your last. I tried this, and all I was left with was a massive hangover, an overdraft and a restraining order banning me from going within five miles of Nicole Kidman.'

To state the obvious, the comedian is exploring the literal reality of living out a bland cliché. Note also, the satisfying triad of thoughts that appear at the end of the joke. It's another version of the 'rule of three', of course. A different comedian on a different day might have chosen to extend the list of things into a huge rant with equal success.

Write down some definitive statements and then see if you can extend their logic into an absurd afterthought. For example, we usually say that we all want a partner with a good sense of humour. What would be the logical outcome of this thought?

That we should all date Coco the Clown? A whoopee cushion on the wedding night? What is *your* answer to these sorts of statements?

The misunderstanding

The misunderstanding is similar to the reversal, but the joke usually revolves around the comedian's stupidity at failing to understand what is really going on. Rather than playfully (or wilfully) switching lanes on the audience's expectations as might happen with a reversal gag, on this occasion it is the comedian's misunderstanding that powers the joke.

Here's a typical misunderstanding joke of Tim Vine's (written, he's asked me to point out, by his sister, Sonya):

> 'So I was getting into my car, and this bloke says to me "Can you give me a lift?" I said, "Sure, you look great, the world's your oyster, go for it."'

Or this joke, which, according to *New Scientist*, was nominated as the world's funniest joke (brace yourself for disappointment):

> 'Two hunters are out in the woods when one of them collapses. He doesn't seem to be breathing and his eyes are rolled back in his head. The other guy whips out his phone and calls the emergency services. He gasps to the operator: "My friend is dead! What can I do?" The operator, in a calm soothing voice, says: "Just take it easy, I can help. First, let's make sure he's dead." There is a silence, and then a shot is heard. The man's voice comes back on line and says: "OK, now what?"'

Try your hand at some misunderstanding jokes. You may already find that you have been creating some when playing some of the afterthought games in this book. But on this occasion, concentrate on really trying to misunderstand everything. Try to turn up the volume on your stupidity dial.

The joke forms listed in the workshop are not meant to confine your creativity. They are certainly not the only way to be funny; neither are they mentioned to try to get you to look or sound like a 'proper stand-up'. They are just some common approaches that comedians have been using for decades, possibly centuries. If you can recognize the underlying mechanism in your joke, then you stand a good chance of being able to replicate it. An inspired amateur may be able to make a group of strangers laugh on occasion; a professional must be able to generate funny material for the rest of their career.

So please treat each of these approaches as a creativity workout for your brain.

Workshop 7: Finding different voices

The human imagination is fantastic. We can conjure up a decades-old argument and rewrite the scene with us saying what we *really* should have said; we can be told a story and feel massive sympathy or hatred for the fictional characters (we may even imbue them with more humanity than we do our neighbours) and we can sum up a complete stranger, at a glance, and make massive assumptions about them from the way they are sitting on a train.

We personalize our universe, window dress it with personalities and attitudes that only exist within the confines of our skulls. There are already a cast of thousands living in our heads before we've even gone out of the front door.

Most of us, when talking to our friends, will 'cartoon' out a scene or facially 'mug' to enhance our story. We will play at being slightly more extreme versions of ourselves or even pretend to be a completely different, distinct personality. Very few of us keep to one voice or character, yet for many new comics this sense of playfulness can evaporate the moment they step on stage.

Are we limiting ourselves by only using our own voice when we are on stage? Should we give some of these other voices in our head free rein?

Exploring stereotypes

We make individual judgements, according to our experience or prejudice, all the time in real life, damning or praising whole groups in society. We may decide that all estate agents are self-serving, or that all car repair people will overcharge or that traffic wardens are the embodiment of pure evil. Clearly, this can't be true. There must be some estate agents who get a kick out of helping both parties or auto mechanics who charge for parts and labour only. But we are happy to use the stereotype as both verbal and social shorthand.

We all do it, but perhaps we're not always aware of doing it. Politicians and newspaper editors exploit this ability we have all the time when they summon up an unlikely Public Enemy Number One, like single mothers ('...destroying the fabric of society!') or football fans ('...evil, lager-swilling, violent scum damaging our reputation abroad!').

No one is a stereotype. But that doesn't stop us from exhibiting the same behaviour that a particular stereotype might on occasion. We can all be as venal as the fictional 'single mum' hate figure, or as boorish as the football lout.

Getting into these other people's minds gives you a better insight into what makes them tick. It brings your target (if you are lampooning this sort of person) into sharper focus. In other words, our greater understanding allows us to become more specific.

Knowledge is power.

Stereotype activities

Summoning up stereotypes

Create a list of innocuous types like 'Supply teacher', 'Junior doctor', 'Vegetarian', 'Real ale supporter' or 'Typical reality TV show contestant' and explore what you think makes them tick. What stereotypical behaviour does each group indulge in? Remember to be specific and, if in doubt, ask yourself questions like:

- What sort of place would they live in?
- Are they in a relationship?
- Where did they last go on holiday?
- What was the last present they received?

Keep answering these questions until you can see this person clearly in your mind.

Try to uncover more about each particular stereotype by playing with your own attitude towards them. The first time you ask questions about them, treat them as a 'hate' figure and go on the attack; the second time, try defending the stereotype – or at least finding the comedian's logical (if twisted) answer to the bad points you previously uncovered about them. For example, you may have initially said (with contempt) that all real ale supporters sport tangled beards, wear pebble glasses and wear massive, oily, Arran jumpers; the second time around, you might defend their dress sense, saying that it's a way for them to recognize each other so that they won't make the mistake of bothering the rest of us.

Inhabiting stereotypes

Once you have explored these 'types' thoroughly, try them on for size. What would your material sound like if it were delivered by an overzealous, 'jobs-worth' traffic warden? What afterthoughts would they add to your jokes? What 'spin' or 'take' would they have on your perceptions? How would a stereotypical vegan deliver material that you've written about holidays abroad, for example?

All these different voices add different 'colours' to your performance palette. If you've uncovered, for example, a particularly anally retentive point of view that helps push the point that you want to make, then *let that voice speak for you*! If these personalities help flesh out the attitudes you are trying to play, then encourage them.

The audience won't think you are weird or self-indulgent: they'll just be carried along by your performance.

As a performer you should encourage yourself to give voice to all these people in your head as they can articulate thoughts or opinions that your everyday self couldn't.

Creating a character act

Sometimes a 'type' will grow and begin to take on a life of its own. You will start to feel so comfortable spouting the fictional character's opinions and your audience will take such delight in hearing the nonsense that they are coming up with, that you may consider developing a character act.

Define the character's limits

A good character act has very set parameters as to what they would and would not do. Their personality is 'set' and the creator should not let the character stray from these limits. For example, if the character is generally intolerant and short tempered, then an audience will only get confused if they start to seem understanding and calm. The creator must stay true to the character and not contradict the reality that they have built up. This is what gives the act its strength. Once the creator is aware of the limits of their character then the material almost seems to write itself. The more extreme those attitudes of the character act become, then the easier it is to generate outrageous afterthoughts. Pick up any newspaper and read out the headlines. What would be your character's comment on them? If you don't know the immediate answer, then you probably haven't firmed up the character enough.

A character act is not just you with a funny voice! It is a completely different personality that you are giving voice to. It is just as 'real' or 'fictional' as the self you present to the everyday world. View the character as a minor form of possession. You are channelling 'its' opinions to the audience. 'It' takes over your body and mouth for 20 minutes.

The character's 'look'

What would your character wear? How would they stand? What is their rhythm of speech? Is it faster or slower than yours? The three stereotype exercises listed above in this workshop will help you find the answers to these questions.

Some comedians can simply put on a pair of glasses to become someone else (like Simon Day's 'Tommy Cockles'), while others need a more complete disguise (in the case of Simon Brodkin's unofficial king of the chavs, Lee 'Nelsy' Nelson). If you choose the latter route, then get used to lugging a big rucksack of costume and props to each performance.

Engaging the audience

The same rules apply to a character act as do to a regular comedian: you are talking *to* an audience, not talking *at* them. In other words, you are not delivering a pre-rehearsed character monologue to the audience; you are interacting with them. You must engage! The single most common error that new character acts commit is failing to reach out to their audience. It is as if they feel that showing off the character is enough. If you know your character inside and out, though, you can deal with any eventuality.

stagecraft

In this chapter you will learn:
- how to present yourself better on stage
- how to deal with nerves
- how to behave onstage and off.

So you've written some material. You've practised it countless times in front of the mirror or to a sympathetic audience if you are working in a group. Now you will want to go out there and see if it works in front of a live crowd. This chapter is devoted to telling you how to present yourself in your best aspect on stage. Obviously, there is no substitution for experience, but hopefully some of the performance tips listed below could shave off some time.

Think about your attitude to your audience

The audience *want* you to succeed. They want to have a good time. They may have had a terrible week and they've come out for a break. They *want* to like you. This is important to remember: new comics can get into a bunker mentality with an audience. They think that if they keep their heads down low and rattle through their material with the minimum of fuss that the whole thing will be over quickly. Think about it: would you like to see someone on stage racing through his or her set, with no breathing space to let the audience in? Of course not. So try to relax and try to make contact with the crowd.

Your jokes, per se, won't save you; but the way you perform those jokes just might. An audience generally want to watch someone who is having a good time; someone who looks like they are in charge.

Remember

You are allowed to feel scared or nervous the first few times. If it was an easy job, everyone would be doing it. But right from the beginning, try to look as if you are enjoying yourself (you probably will after your first laugh…).

Treat the audience exactly how you would treat your friends

• Relax and take your time.
• Don't assume a defensive posture (don't let your shoulders creep up, for example).

- Don't become so rigid in your body posture that you look like you are a rabbit trapped in the headlights. (A great trick that comedian Martin Beaumont always advises is to try to imagine your best friend's head on the shoulders of each audience member.)
- Give the audience the benefit of the doubt and assume the best.
- Adopt the same body language that you would share with your best friends. This means far more than the simple command of 'show no fear'; it means you should positively encourage the audience to think you are having a good time with them. Body language is a strange thing: even if the audience does seem a little cold or hostile (which hardly ever happens), then the simple act of faking having a good time can warm them up until you begin to find that you are *actually* enjoying yourself.

Be warned: If you go on stage with the attitude that it is going to be an uphill struggle, you will probably be creating a self-fulfilling prophecy.

Force yourself to look at the audience

Make eye contact, if you can see them; stare at their vague outlines if you can't.

Many newer comics make the mistake of staring over the heads of the audience because they worry that the crowd will distract them but, in actual fact, all they are doing is distancing themselves from their audience. They are failing to make contact. They are setting up an artificial barrier between them and the people they are trying to entertain. Similarly, some comics will stare at the ground, thinking that this will help them remember what comes next. Or they will look down after a punchline because they think this punctuates their performance, when all it does is make them look abashed. Looking over or 'under' the audience's heads are both big mistakes for a performer to make. *Look at the crowd.* You'll seem much more human to them if you do.

Try to 'read' the crowd

To some extent the audience subtly direct your performance; that is to say, even though your material might not change from night to night, your delivery will alter – ever so slightly – by the different dynamics of each audience. If you don't look at them, you can't learn to 'read' them. Metaphorically, you should feel that you are having a dialogue with the audience, even though it seems like a monologue. So let them in. You are not just reciting jokes. You are telling them your thoughts; and just like you would with your friends, you are checking in with them now and then to see if they are still with you. This can only be done if you look at them!

When you are looking at the audience, scan them all. Don't fixate on the one person yawning or the couple who don't laugh at your best joke (it's easy to focus on the glum faces to the exclusion of all else, especially when you start out) and don't assume that the audience can spot any mistake you make. If you skip a bit, let yourself off the hook; the audience have no idea what you are going to say next, and they certainly don't care about the wonderfully clever set construction that you've come up with. All they want to do is have a good laugh at your material.

All the adrenaline rushing through your body at the first few gigs will make the whole experience become a bit of a blur: you'll probably feel like you've just bungee jumped when you come off stage and have no clear idea of what you did or didn't do. But after a while, being on stage begins to seem a little less strange and at that point you can start processing all the information coming in to your brain. Then you can *really* start to work on your relationship with the audience.

Slow down!

The first few times on stage, with all the excitement and all the nerves, will set your mind racing. This usually translates physically into the comedian rushing through their set at 90 miles per hour. If the newer comic ever rationalizes his or her behaviour (which they rarely do) they might think that the quicker they get to their punchlines, the more the audience will laugh. But remember, we are not in the business of 'just' telling jokes: we are giving the audience a performance. You cannot inhabit your material and successfully play with all the attitudes you wish to adopt if you are rushing through everything. A joke shouldn't just be timed by the mere seconds it takes to tell it: it should be timed by the amount of time it takes to tell it *and the reaction time the audience need to understand it and start laughing*. If you are racing through your set and failing to acknowledge the audience, then you are not really doing your job.

As a new comic, all you have to do is make the audience laugh fairly regularly for five minutes or ten minutes. You will do this much more successfully if you try to relax and make a conscious effort to slow down. The trap that a lot of new comedians fall into at the very beginning of their career is trying to cram their allotted time with too many jokes. This means they have to race through their set, giving the audience no time to laugh and certainly no time to enjoy themselves. This is something that I was guilty of the first couple of years of my career: I had so much that I wanted to say that I would rush through all my stuff and step on the audience's laughter, impatient to get on to the next bit. Then I watched how more experienced comics would often leave a beat or even a small pause after a funny bit and give the audience time to laugh *as much as they wanted*. I tried it myself and discovered that lines that were only going down moderately well before were now getting much bigger laughs – on some nights they even got a round of applause. To state the obvious, a pause not only allows the audience to acknowledge a good joke and show their appreciation, it can also give you time for a further reaction shot to your own material – the audience can watch your thoughts play across your face.

Speeding through your set means that inevitably your timing will be off

The rhythm will be wrong and unnatural and therefore it will be harder for the audience to grasp your ideas. Perhaps a good way for you to think about comic timing is to consider it as the amount of time you need to show the audience the thought process that leads you to your punchline. Too little time and they won't understand you as much as you may want them to; too much time and the audience have got there before you and think that you are a bit slow.

How to deal with nerves

Eventually, with time and experience, stage nerves fade away to nothing. But at the beginning of your career, they can be crippling. Strangely, the terror that some acts feel seems to evaporate with the first laugh from the audience. Perhaps we exacerbate the problem by giving these nerves the scary title of 'Stage fright'. Let's look at the phenomenon more closely.

Before a show, some comedians feel their heart start to race; their limbs become all twitchy; the mouth goes dry; they feel the need to empty their bladders a million times before they go on stage or they may feel wound up tighter than a watch spring. To give some sort of form to all these strange sensations they tell themselves they are starting to feel fear. At this point, having given the feelings a handy title, the individual comic may feel an overriding desire to either run away or just get on stage and get it all over with. The longer they have to wait, the more the body starts behaving at fever pitch.

May I suggest that what the comedian is feeling at these points isn't actually fear? What they are experiencing is a release of adrenaline into their bodies. The comedian is gearing up to go out on stage and to work at their peak. But, unfortunately, we are all victims of our animal ancestry and our previous experiences. The last time, off stage, that any of us felt an adrenaline rush was probably in the school playground when we were about to get picked on and a 'fight or flight' response was triggered; or perhaps some idiot persuaded us to go skydiving and our bodies – not realising that this death-defying stunt was supposed to be fun – tried to find some way to escape the situation and triggered an adrenal response. So we are 'trained' to think that every time we feel adrenaline that we must either punch someone or run away. Clearly, neither response would help our comedy careers.

But adrenaline isn't just about 'fight or flight'; luckily, we are slightly more sophisticated creatures than our ancestors were. The modern world asks us to make much more sophisticated choices than either 'kill it' or 'run away'! But our muscle memory accesses all the previous times we've felt adrenaline, and told us to treat stepping onto the stage in the same way we treated the school yard or skydiving experience.

Try telling yourself that what you are feeling isn't fear, it is simply adrenaline. You have the freedom to classify the feeling any way you want. You can say it is fear. But you can also say (far more constructively, perhaps) that your body is gearing up to work at 110 per cent. You are probably feeling the same way that athletes feel before an important event. Would they describe their state as fear? Probably not. Adrenaline will help to make you work at full capacity. It is the thing that will make your brain sharper and your reactions quicker. It makes you *shine*. It will make your normal, everyday self seem like a slow, plodding workhorse.

So when you first begin to feel your heart race, recognize it for what it actually is and embrace the feeling. *Adrenaline is your friend.*

Before a gig, make time for you

Feel free to stretch, yawn, pace up and down – do whatever you can to shake the chinks out of your body and the cobwebs out of your head. But don't feel you have to do it in public. You can always lock yourself in a lavatory cubicle or take a walk around the block (make sure you're back in good time, though).

Don't get sidetracked

Don't allow another comic to collar you if you want some time by yourself. No one will think you rude if you want to be by yourself or in your own world. We have all been there. I once worked with a very famous singer and his way of 'gearing up' for a performance was to talk (incessantly!) to anyone who would listen. If you were foolish enough to make eye contact, that was it, you were trapped! His talking helped him, but it did nothing for the other acts on the bill who were stuck with him. Should anybody try to monopolize your time when you have some preparation to do, just make your excuses and go. They probably won't even notice.

Some basic things that a comedian can do to steady themselves before a show and to 'ground' themselves are:

- Take a few deep, slow breaths. Concentrate on the exhale. Push all the air out of your lungs and (because nature abhors a vacuum) let your lungs, naturally and freely, suck in all that wonderful fresh air. Don't overdo it though, and make yourself dizzy.
- Bend your knees ever so gently while standing and relax your upper body (especially the shoulders). Be aware of the massive weight of meat and bone that you are. Feel how heavy you are against the ground. Often nerves can make us live entirely in our head, so anything you can do to remind yourself of the marvellous body you carry around with you can only be a good thing.

- Lean against a wall, as if you were doing a press-up or two, to push some blood back into your arms.
- Try to keep fluid in your movements: rigidity breeds tension.
- Most importantly: TELL YOURSELF YOU ARE GOING TO HAVE A GOOD TIME. Even the scariest roller-coaster ride in the world is fun!

It all seems very strange when you step on stage for the very first time because you don't know what to expect. But this feeling will soon change.

The only certainty you can ever have is that the experience will always be completely different from how you imagined; so keep your eyes and ears open and try to enjoy yourself.

Don't drink

Or take any drugs. They won't make you any funnier. Or any more relaxed. They will just slow you down and make it harder for you to read the audience. The best drug in the world is being on stage! Trust me. Roger Daltrey said it was better than sex. I would qualify that and say that it is better than bad sex...

Your only relationship is with the audience

When working, try to remember that your primary focus isn't trying to impress other comics or even the promoter of the club. All your energy should be devoted to the audience. They are the only ones who matter. So banish that weird little comment or look that a fellow comedian gave you before you went on stage (it's probably paranoia, anyway); forget any arguments you had with a loved one during the day or any worries that have been burdening you throughout the week. Your only loyalty, whilst you are on stage, is to the audience. Treat them with all the attention you would give someone on a first date.

Familiarity breeds content(ment)

Know your stuff backwards. The more you rehearse your material and the more familiar you are with it, the more you can, paradoxically, play around with it. The more you know your material, the more fully you will begin to inhabit it.

Know the room. Become familiar with it. Stand at the back. Will audience members standing there be able to see everything? Are there any places with a restricted view?

Get to the venue and check everything out. Forewarned is forearmed. Ask to check out the microphone before the audience is let in: never assume that someone has done a sound check if you weren't there to witness it. It may happen at the bigger clubs, but a handful of the smaller ones are run very shambolically. The promoter of the club is completely within his or her rights to refuse you this courtesy but, at the very least, ask to stand on the stage so that you can check out sightlines and dark spots.

Try to tape yourself at every gig

If you audio-record every performance, you will have an objective record of what you have done. This can be invaluable for a variety of reasons:

- First and foremost, it can record spontaneity: any funny thoughts that spring from your mouth will probably be lost forever if you don't record yourself. Don't expect other comedians to remember any new funny bits you've come up with; don't expect any friends in the audience to either. Tape yourself and insure yourself against a fallible memory.
- Similarly, often your mouth, in the heat of the moment, will find a much more concise way of saying something than your conscious brain did when originally writing the thoughts. A recording will capture the new rhythm or wording exactly.
- Taping the gig might explain why a usually solid joke went down less than well. Did the wording change without you being aware? Did an argument begin at a table near the back, which you were unaware of at the time, managing to upstage your punchline?

Run through a list of your material immediately after the gig

Try to go through your set and analyse as soon as you can after coming off stage. Certainly try to do it before you go to bed, especially if you haven't taped your performance. If you wait for the next day you will only have a vague recollection of how it went down.

What worked well? What didn't? What could you do to improve it? Were there any improvized bits that are worth incorporating into the act or were they only 'one-offs' that wouldn't work with a different crowd?

A little bit of critical appraisal will go a long way in this business and help you become a much better comedian more quickly.

Sell yourself on stage

Put your best foot forward and give the audience the best show you can do. Ask yourself what you would expect from the best performer in the world, then try to emulate that.

Try to dazzle the audience. Be in control, without appearing to be arrogant (unless you are 'playing' arrogant). Be confident, but not cocky (unless you're 'playing' cocky).

Audiences want to be reassured. They want to feel that you are in control. They have paid good money to sit in a warm, cosy, dark space and abdicate all responsibility to *you*. So, be in charge.

Let us finish this chapter with one final caveat:

NEVER EVER try new material at a gig that could lead to you getting a paid gig.

At the beginning of your career you will be asked to do countless five minute 'open spot' performances at comedy clubs. In effect, you are auditioning in front of a live audience. The club promoter wants to see if you are funny or not. If they like you enough, they may ask you back to do more, with the eventual aim of being hired to do a longer set. Given this, you owe it to yourself to always present your best ideas in front of that particular audience. So resist the urge to sneak in that very funny new routine that you came up with three hours ago, rather than the tried and tested (and also honed and polished) material you usually do.

09 microphone technique

In this chapter you will learn:
- how to approach the microphone confidently
- how to maximize your performance through the microphone
- how to avoid pitfalls with the mike stand.

The quality of microphone varies enormously from venue to venue. Some are state of the art and some, quite frankly, make the comedian sound as if he or she is talking through wet wool. That is why it's advisable to have a thorough sound check at every venue you perform in. At university gigs and at the bigger venues this won't be a problem; the sound technician will be only too happy to let you have a test run with their kit. At the smaller, less well-organized gigs, you may find that the club promoter hasn't left enough setting up time before they have to let the audience in for you to have a go. Even so, try to insist on a quick practise before the audience come in. But be nice about it! These are the people who book you.

During the check, run through a couple of different lines from your set. Be as loud as you would hope to be on stage. Put the mike down and talk loudly. Does the room soak up the sound? Do you do anything weird vocally? If so, try it out. Work out how to adjust the mike to your height. If you are going to do it, practise taking the mike out of the stand. Is the lead firmly attached to the microphone? Most importantly, though, spend a couple of moments behind the mike and try to get a feel for the room.

Microphone mistakes

Here are a few simple microphone mistakes that you should avoid making.

Don't rush to the mike stand

Take time to establish your presence. Act as if you have a perfect right to be there. Don't run on and start talking to the audience when you are still several feet from the stand. People do this out of some sense of fear that if they don't start immediately that the audience will decide to wander off to the bar. If you do this you will just create a mad chaos of movement and sound and look like you are panicked or unfocused. An old Zen saying seems particularly appropriate to remember when you are thinking about taking to the stage:

> 'When walking, just walk. When sitting, just sit. But above all don't wobble!'

In other words, walk to the microphone *then* start talking. Behave like someone who feels confident (and *is* confident!) rather than someone trying not to trip over their own feet.

Don't get too close to the mike

A lot of new comedians make the mistake of thinking that being louder equates with being better. So often they will practically have their lips kissing the mike. This is too close. Similarly, some comedians will rest it on their chin as they think this will mean that (a) they're loud enough and (b) they can forget about the microphone for the rest of the show. Both these approaches are wrong. You may sound louder, but you will probably sound more distorted too. Some comics never consider that the audience may be struggling to understand what is being said. Also, resting the mike on the chin means that the comedian is lumbered with a 'one size fits all' default volume. A good mike should always be five or six inches away from the face and positioned slightly below the mouth (to prevent loud percussive 'poppings' with plosive consonants). But, given the variable state of comedy club microphones, treat this as a friendly suggestion rather than a golden rule. A microphone should never be up against the face unless you are whispering something into it, pretending to become intimate or using its proximity to emphasize a particular phrase. Remember, if it is hiding half your face, then it is obscuring at least half of your facial expressions too.

Don't be too far away

Some beginners let the hand holding the mike sag to their lower chest or even their belly. Obviously, the only thing the microphone will pick up at this level is possibly the sound of your digestion.

Don't hunch over the mike stand

Get it to your level. Don't lean into it. You must look like you are comfortable on stage, not practising extreme yoga.

Don't treat the microphone gingerly

Be confident. The mike is not your enemy, it won't betray you; it is just an instrument to help you communicate your thoughts to a large room. So don't fixate on it, you should be focusing on your audience.

Don't play with the mike lead

It distracts. Obviously, there are exceptions. Woody Allen used to wrap the mike lead around his body in a way that suggested he was half treating it like a security blanket and half trying to strangle himself. This suited his uber-neurotic persona. For most of us, though, it just looks like we are fiddling.

Also, don't hold the wire up in front of you – it looks like you are trying to create a barrier between you and the audience.

Mike – in the stand or the hand?

There is no common consensus as to whether or not you should take the mike out of the stand or not. One stance is not considered more 'professional' than the other. It's really just a matter of what suits your temperament. Once you have decided which you prefer, try to stick to it for the rest of your set. Don't keep popping it back in and out of the stand for no good reason. It is just another distraction and will irritate.

If you prefer to hold a mike in your hand, make sure you have a good idea of what to do with the mike stand. Just pick it up and put it behind you, out of the way where it won't create a barrier between you and the crowd.

Once you have the mike in your hand, one handy tip is to loop a coil of lead nearest the microphone around the hand holding it. That can prevent the lead jack being inadvertently pulled loose should you accidentally step on it. It can also make you look a little like Tom Jones singing in Las Vegas, so don't make the loop too ostentatious.

When you are wrapping up your set, grab the mike stand and place it back in front of you before you attempt to put the microphone back in the stand. That way, you'll never have your back to the audience and also you will have given the MC a clear signal that you are about to close your set. You leave the stage exactly as you find it, with the mike in the stand, centre stage, in a neutral starting position, ready for the next act.

Remember

The more practice you get with the microphone, the more competent a stand-up you will become. Eventually it will become second nature to you.

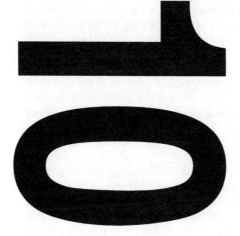

10

hecklers and crowd control

In this chapter you will learn:
- what makes a good gig and a bad gig
- tips for dealing with difficult audiences
- how to deal with hecklers.

Most new acts worry about being heckled or otherwise abused by the crowd. This is possibly because a very primitive part of our brain isn't entirely comfortable about being the only single 'lit' target in a room full of strangers. But the truth is, you will probably be heckled a lot less than you ever imagined you would be. Most audience members don't want to draw attention to themselves: they've just come for a good night out and want *you* to do the talking. As long as you are keeping an audience laughing, then there is no need for them to begin feeling restless. Hopefully, you will have peppered your routine with lots of afterthought gags and asides, which are designed to illicit laughter with a certain frequency. You may even decide to start your set by hitting them hard with four or five rapid, sure-fire jokes that prove to the audience that (a) you are funny and (b) they can relax, knowing that they are in good hands. If you launch into a long lecture with no punchline in sight, I'm afraid you only have yourself to blame.

Remember, the longer the set up, the funnier the punchline has to be...

Why a gig can go bad

Having said that, sometimes events can slip out of your control. Often this can be because you are ignoring the needs of the crowd. Perhaps a group start talking and you don't have the nerve to address the situation; perhaps you are staring above the audience's head, desperately trying to remember what comes next, and they start to lose interest in you because you don't seem terribly interested in them; perhaps the audience have got in for free and have no emotional investment in the evening, or half the audience is resentful that 'their' pub has been taken over by a bunch of show-offs.

Preparation can prevent a lot of bad situations arising. If you are at the venue from the very start of the evening, then you can often anticipate some problem areas. Is one group a little bit chatty, but essentially harmless? If you come to the gig late, you may not know this and slap them down too hard when all they are doing is agreeing with you. Is the sound system appalling and are the audience too busy straining to hear than to concentrate on laughing? Has a row kicked off in the first half of the show among a party in the audience that you, as a latecomer, are unaware of? These scenarios, and others like them, are few and far between but a little bit of preparation (turning up early, doing a sound check, standing on stage and getting a feel for the room, standing at the back and soaking up the audience 'vibe') will go a long way to putting you more in control of the room.

How to make a gig better

When you are on stage there are a number of things you can encourage yourself to do to make yourself seem more in charge.

> As a general rule: fake having a good time until your brain lets go and you actually start enjoying yourself.

Make contact

Look at the crowd. Connect with them. Remember to smile (unless it really doesn't fit your style). Take your time; don't race through it. Don't focus on one group: spread your attention amongst the whole audience. Don't ask a barrage of pointless questions like 'How are we all doing tonight?' or 'Is this mike on?' or 'Didn't you get that bit?' unless you have a very funny afterthought to back it up with; otherwise you are wasting the audience's time.

Remember to visually 'check in' with your audience all the time. Use all the social skills you have to make the audience members feel 'special'. This last suggestion is by nature a little vague as we all have slightly different ways of interacting with each other – but a general warning would be not to behave as a bore at a party who will drone on about his or her life and not let anyone else into the experience. You must let the audience in!

Drawing the audience in

If you are confident enough, you could always drag individual members of the audience into your own personal soap opera. If three or four men are sitting together, then obviously (in your mind) they've all been dumped and have come out to take their minds off the tragic mess they've made of their lives; if you are corrected on a point of information by a member of the audience, then clearly that person becomes the supply teacher in the room. A young couple become star-crossed lovers, or a couple having an affair, or the man is offering his partner a cheapskate night out – wouldn't she rather be at a restaurant? Is it a first date? Then why did he bring her to a place where they couldn't talk? Playing with the audience in this manner may seem very scary at first – however, it doesn't have to be. At the first sign of trouble you can simply return to your material. But it can also be very rewarding and it's also a very good way of drawing an audience in.

Preparing the ground for audience participation

Are you the sort of comic who likes to asks individual audience members questions? If you are, why not save yourself some trouble and have some pre-prepared answers up your sleeve? For example, if you were to ask a man and woman sitting together if they were a couple, why not have a funny response ready for both a 'yes' and a 'no' answer? With a little bit of preparation, you could work out a branching diagram of most of the probable things that individuals might say in response to your inquiries, which will make the audience think that you are an improvising genius rather than just being an extremely hard working comedian who has done his or her homework.

Is the venue set up to allow you to win?

One final word before we move onto dealing with hecklers: sometimes a show can go pear-shaped because of circumstances completely beyond your control. Often, if a venue has a bad reputation, it's usually because there is a fundamental mistake with the layout of the venue. Perhaps the audience are too brightly lit and feel too exposed; perhaps there is a gap between the stage and the audience area that regular punters use to get to the loos – all that passing traffic won't help focus an audience's attention; or perhaps there are obscuring pillars that restrict some of the audience's view.

We only need two simple factors to create a good venue: we need an audience to feel they are being treated like an audience and we need a space for the performers to shine in. If one of these two things is missing or fudged then the space is not a performance space – at best, the comedians will stumble through; although the worst case scenario could mean that may become a bear pit.

If you find yourself standing in the corner of a function room above a pub, with a useless mike, an angle-poise lamp for lighting and peeling wallpaper for a backdrop, then chances are you will have an uphill battle. If this is the case, can you completely blame yourself for a bad gig?

Hecklers

Being barracked by members of the audience usually only happens because of one of two reasons: either *you have lost the interest of the audience* or the heckler is an idiot. Let's look at both scenarios.

You have lost the interest of the audience

And they, in turn, have lost patience with you. If this is the case, you've probably not paid attention to earlier warning signs, like an ominous silence building or more people going to the bar when they should be paying attention to you. In this case all you can do is try to win back their trust and vow to learn from the mistakes you have made that lead to them turning against you. If it starts to go *really* badly, all you can do is try to acknowledge the situation, and either change tack (they're obviously not big fans of your present subject matter) or get off stage with as much good will as you can possibly muster. Don't be tempted to go over your allotted time with the seductive, egotistical argument that: 'If I do just one more bit, I'll be able to win them back...' You won't. If the audience has made a collective decision that you are wasting their time, you will rarely win them back. Better to stop, try to figure out what went wrong and move on to the next gig.

The person heckling you is an idiot

Nine times out of ten you will be interrupted by some idiot who clearly didn't get enough attention when they were a child, or who is drunk or trying to impress someone. But this sort of heckler is at a huge disadvantage for a number of reasons: the rest of the audience wants them to shut up, they've paid good money and they don't want it ruined by someone who is being disruptive. Also, the heckler is usually drunk, so your sober self can run rings around them. Remember too, that you are the one holding the microphone so, to a very large extent, you control the situation.

You have the choice as a comedian of either learning some standard heckler put-downs like 'I remember my first drink, as well' or 'Don't tell me how to do my job! Otherwise I'll follow you to work tomorrow and interrupt YOU just as you're asking the customer if they want fries with that?'

Or you could take the much more rewarding path of just relying on your wits to answer whatever they have thrown at you. There is no shame in throwing an old line at an audience member if it shuts him or her up, but you will gain more kudos from your fellow comics if you make up something on the spot.

Here are some basic ground rules when dealing with the idiot heckler.

- **Don't panic!** Remember that you are in charge and that everyone wants you to win.
- **Repeat what the heckler has said.** This is so that everyone can hear what has been said. You may have the best come back in the world, but if we don't hear the heckle, it won't make any sense. Repeating the heckle also gives you breathing time to think of a snappy afterthought. Sometimes the very fact of you repeating what they say can show up the stupidity or illogicality in their suggestion.
- **Pretend to not hear and get them to repeat the heckle again (and even again).** This diminishes the impact and hopefully makes the heckler look a little foolish.
- **If you can't understand what they're saying, then repeat what you *think* they are hearing and mock that.**
- **Never get angry.** It's not your ego on the line. It will only make the audience think that perhaps the heckler is getting to you and they will wonder what happened to the nice comedian who was entertaining them only minutes before. Never get into a shouting match with a member of the audience – you will always lose. Keep everything light and airy. Give the impression that you are tolerating the heckler, even though everyone else in the room hates him or her.
- **As a last resort, if they won't shut up, then try invoking democracy and get the audience to tell them to shut up.** By this stage, the management should have had a word with them. But if the club is not particularly well run, then you will have to take charge.

Crowd control exercises

Here are some crowd control exercises. You'll need a group for both of these, to mimic dealing with an audience.

MC in hell

(A group game: the larger the group the better!)

One of you will be the MC who is going to introduce the best act in the world; another person in the group is going to be the stage manager who oversees the game. The rest of the group are playing an impatient and 'bolshy' audience.

The MC will whip the crowd up and give the act a really good introduction – but just as they are about to bring them on stage, the stage manager will whisper in the MC's ear that the act is delayed…

So of course, the MC must try to cover this minor hiccup until the act is ready. Eventually, the stage manager lets the MC know that the act really *is* ready this time; once again the act is introduced, but yet again, at the last moment, the stage manager makes up some excuse for a delay (perhaps they are locked in a lavatory, or stuck in traffic). Once again, the MC must try to placate the crowd, who at this point might start to become a tad restless. This false start is repeated again and again, with the 'crowd' getting more vociferous with each disappointment. The pattern is repeated until the MC is at the end of their tether.

The exercise can never replace the experience of going down with all guns blazing, but it can give a taste of what it's like.

The minister's press conference

Each person takes turns in answering questions at a press conference from the rest of the group who are posing as journalists. (If you can use a microphone and a mike stand for this game, so much the better.) They must each be made the head of some ridiculous ministry, perhaps the 'Ministry for Monkeys (but not Apes)' or the 'Ministry for Putting Things into Other Things' or the 'Ministry for Sharpening Sticks'. Then with great authority they must try to answer all of the questions that the press ask them. The minister must not bat the question away: they are the expert and must try to answer the question to everyone's satisfaction. This exercise is great practice for the individual comic to come up with ideas 'on the hoof'.

The rest of the group must have their hands raised at all times, ready to ask a probing question. They should feel free to be as caustic, grovelling or sly as they want to be. Often the journalists will try to ensnare the minister in some scandal or fake some national outrage to get a reaction from the minister.

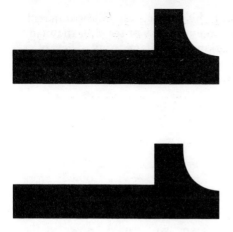

11

what other comics think

In this chapter you will learn:
- what tips professional comics have to offer
- what are the best and worst things about this job
- how comedians structure their working day.

Every comedian's approach to his or her craft will be different. With that in mind, here are the opinions of some of the many professional comedians working in Britain today. They offer their tips, their warnings and any advice that they can think of. They occasionally swear, too. You have been warned.

Milton Jones

Milton Jones is the star of six radio series for Radio 4. He won the Time Out *Comedy Award in 2003. A former Perrier Best Newcomer Award winner and nominee, he is a Comedy Store regular and has been described as 'King of the surreal one-liners' in* The Times.

What do you know now that you wish you'd known at the beginning of your career?
That it's a game of Snakes and Ladders, and that you have to learn how to climb up a snake.

Did you ever have a 'eureka' moment in your career when things fell into place? If so, what?
Treating my stage persona as a 'character' helped me find a style of writing and performing.

What is the best thing about this job?
Free time during the day. And going to interesting places and meeting interesting people.

What's the worst thing about this job?
Going to uninteresting places and meeting uninteresting people.

What would be a typical working day for you?
Morning 9–12: write/admin; afternoon off; evening 7.30–12.30: gig/s (depending on travel).

What makes a good gig?
Trying something new that works: written or improvized.

What makes a bad gig?
An indifferent audience.

Any tips on dealing with hecklers?
Relax: try and give them enough rope to hang themselves (e.g. ask them a question; if they are funny, acknowledge it).

What advice would you offer someone starting out in this business?
Give it 100% for two years. If you give less, you will never know what you could have achieved.

Do as much as you can.

Try to shrug off both abuse and applause.

Richard Herring

Richard has worked as a comic, a writer and devised and performed in highly acclaimed one-man shows at the Edinburgh Festival. He has a large student following and was one half of the Sunday morning TV comedy show Good Morning with Richard, not Judy, *along with Stewart Lee.*

What do you know now that you wish you'd known at the beginning of your career?
I wish I had known loads of things.

I wish I had known that I could be good at this job. I lacked the confidence to be a really effective stand-up when I started, did a couple of variable years and then convinced myself I was only any good working with other people. It took me a long time to realize that I could perform alone and even longer to try to be a stand-up again. I suppose part of the problem with starting this job in your early 20s is that you have comparatively little experience and perspective of life – not to say there aren't some great young comedians, but we hopefully get better with age. But I think that generally confidence is the key thing in becoming an effective stand-up and maybe if I had known that 20 years ago, I would have done more stand-up earlier.

I wish I had realized that it is better to persevere with the things that you think are funny than try to tailor your act into what you imagine the club owners want. In the long run you will succeed when you find your own voice and I think my original act was a bit of a hotchpotch as I struggled to combine both things I liked and things that I thought might get me work.

Did you ever have a 'eureka' moment in your career when things fell into place? If so, what?
Not exactly, but I suppose the realization a couple of years ago that the stage shows I was doing were not a million miles from

stand-up was a big moment. I had a tough time with stand-up in the early years and it was a big step for me to face my demons and go back to it. I had been humiliated many times and convinced myself I wasn't cut out for it. So having the courage to try again was a big step, as was the decision to take some risks and try less accessible material and I suppose not care if the audiences and promoters didn't like it. As it turned out they mainly did, but it was learning to trust myself that took me forwards. It's not that you don't care at all: it's just that you aren't fretting about what the reaction is. It's self-belief and confidence again. These are qualities that weirdly the best and the worst acts seem to share.

What is the best thing about this job?
Loads of good stuff. When it's working out for you and you're on stage and the audience are with you and you're freewheeling to a point where even you're not sure what's coming out of your mouth next, and the stuff that comes out turns out to be a brilliantly funny improvized routine, then it's hard to get a better feeling. When you have an audience crying with laughter and in pain and you know you've got something funnier coming up – that is also an extraordinary feeling (doesn't happen too often, I have to say). It's such a privilege to get paid for doing something that is generally terrific fun and on the great nights you have a brilliant gig and then you have some drinks after and adventures happen. At times like this it's hard to imagine a better way to make a living.

What's the worst thing about this job?
The gigs where your ad libs come out wrong and the audience doesn't like you and you come off feeling like you're the least funny man in the world do counterbalance the good ones (even though they happen a lot less). A bad gig or even a mediocre one where you know you haven't been on top of your game can make you feel awful. And it's a bit crap that the way a gig goes (either good or bad) can affect your mood for days. Often being on the road is not as much fun as you might hope or as people imagine. You find yourself alone in hotel bars quite a lot, unable to sleep as you're still running on adrenaline. Or you have a long drive home and don't get to bed until 3.00 or 4.00am which can screw up your day and your mood. It can get a bit lonely and depressing and the difference between the false euphoria of being on stage and the reality of the off stage world can sometimes jar a little.

Pricks in the audience who ruin a great gig that everyone else is loving by refusing to shut up even when you have done a brilliant job in putting them down.

Loads of bad things too, but on the whole I think the positives far outweigh the negatives, even if I could write a lot more about the negatives!

What would be a typical working day for you?
There isn't really a typical one. Or maybe the typical day is one like today where I prevaricate and get nothing done.

I try to write in the daytime. Sometimes this goes well, but mainly I end up achieving nothing and feeling miserable with myself. I spend a lot of time dicking around on the Internet. Then it depends if I am gigging and how far away the gig is. But like I've said, if it's a few hours drive away then I can be out until the early hours.

I do write a weblog every day at some point, which for the last four years has been my one regular activity, but I do it at different times of the day, so even that is not typical. The only time I get into a definite routine is in Edinburgh, where I do my show, get drunk, go to bed at about 4.00am, sleep in until about 2.00pm, watch TV, do my show again and repeat x 24.

What makes a good gig?
As I said above I suppose it's when you as a performer reach that point where you are freewheeling and the audience are going with you and there's a palpable atmosphere of excitement that does almost feel like electricity. It's rare, but it's great when you get the kind of audience that are chipping in with things that are adding to the set: either a good question or a funny extension of something – trying to add to what you're doing, rather than knocking you down.

What makes a bad gig?
Again covered a bit above. It's hard to be sure. Sometimes it's your fault. Sometimes your timing is off or your attitude is wrong. Sometimes you get the wrong kind of crowd for your kind of material. Sometimes there are just idiots in the audience who are determined to ruin everything. I get more upset by the ones where I screw up though; but screwing up is all part of the learning process and I think you have to constantly push at your own boundaries and experiment with how you do things and this does mean that occasionally you say the wrong thing or come across looking like a dick. It hurts for a bit. You get over it. Especially after a good gig. Comedians are nothing if not shallow.

Any tips on dealing with hecklers?

Though it's good to have a few prepared lines, I think it's generally best to deal with each situation as it comes. You will look cleverer and sharper if you are responding honestly and instinctively to what is going on, rather than falling back on stock lines. It's risky, of course, as you might not come up with stuff, but ultimately it doesn't matter too much what you say as long as you remain in control. Coming back with something fast and measured is probably the best thing. But you have to keep your cool and the minute you lose your temper (which is very easy to do and I do it myself still every now and again) you have lost it. Sometimes you can pretend to lose your temper and it will work, but only if you are ultimately in control. Occasionally losing it can work for you, but it's a risky strategy.

Most hecklers are drunk and useless and not as funny as you and the majority of the audience probably hates them. Use that against them. Usually most people will be on your side and a well-timed barb will be enough to get you their laughter and their respect. Dealing well with a heckler can turn an ordinary gig into a brilliant one as people do seem to have a lot of respect for material they perceive as being off the cuff. If the whole crowd is booing you, then it's harder, but if you keep fighting you can sometimes win them back. Confidence and self-belief will do a lot to help you as in every other aspect of this job. Don't show weakness and don't feel you always have to come straight back with something. A weighted pause followed by a considered and funny response can often kill a heckler dead. It's just about showing you're the boss. They can smell your fear (occasionally literally) so you must not give them any opportunity to sense it.

What advice would you offer someone starting out in this business?

Try again; fail again; fail better.

Every gig is a learning experience. Experiment with stuff. I have managed to find new jokes or a new intonation or change of a word that suddenly makes a joke or routine better on the 200th time I've done it.

You really just need to get as much stage time as you possibly can. The more you gig the better you will get.

Also, though there is a chance that you are not as funny as you hope. There is always time to improve and no one steps up on stage and is just brilliant straightaway. But don't keep plugging

way at this job if it really is never working for you. I would set
time limit of, say, maybe five years; if you find that audiences
till don't like you and promoters don't want to book you then
could be time to think about doing something else. Most
people come to realize this themselves; but even though it takes
time to become funny, there are some people who are not cut
out for this unusual job.

Good luck though. A trail of tears of misery and joy lay in front
of you. It's a spectacular way to make a living, and at its best is
a lot of fun.

Steve Hall

*Steve Hall has worked all over the country and in Europe. He is
one third of the acclaimed comedy group 'We are Klang'.*

**What do you know now that you wish you'd known at the
beginning of your career?**
That the girl I'd meet after that gig in Glasgow only had one eye.

**Did you ever have a 'eureka' moment in your career when things
fell into place? If so, what?**
Things only fall into place as a result of consistent hard work
over a long period of time. I think eureka moments are illusory:
a really good gig can leave you convinced you can do no wrong,
only for the next night to find yourself looking like a mentally
ill person holding a microphone. The harder you work, the
more consistently well you'll hopefully find yourself doing. So
you can end up with a feeling of general contentment that you
make a living at this strange and wonderful business – whereas
what you might perceive to be an individual eureka moment
usually precedes something going soul-shatteringly tits-up.

What is the best thing about this job?
Comparing it to what I did before.

What's the worst thing about this job?
Other than the desperate feeling of isolation; the conviction that
you're going to get found out as a fraud at any moment; the
fractured lifestyle; boredom of travelling and the unwanted
feelings of ravenous competitiveness towards your peers, this a
job with no down side.

What makes a good gig?
Doing well.

What makes a bad gig?
Sucking.

Any tips on dealing with hecklers?
Context is vital, so go to different sorts of clubs and see the various methods used to deal with hecklers, and think how you'd handle that situation.

Sarah Kendal

Sarah has been doing stand-up for about eight years and lived in Britain for six. In that time she has been nominated for both the Perrier and Time Out *Comedy Award. A regular at the Edinburgh Comedy Festival, she has performed all over the place: Hong Kong, South Africa, Belgium, Holland, Germany, New York, Norway and Luton.*

What do you know now that you wish you'd known at the beginning of your career?
In spite of the way your body might be reacting, there's nothing to be afraid of. I used to get crippling nerves – my hands would shake so badly I couldn't bring myself to even try and take the mike out of the stand. I'd sweat and my mouth would be bone dry. I spent years overcoming my nerves.

I think most of the fear response is driven by the idea that something terrible is going to happen if you don't have a good gig. After doing it for years and experiencing all kinds of audiences, you realize that it's okay if you have a bad gig. It's okay to fail. There are some nights when it's your fault and you just did a bad show; there are other nights when the crowd is crap. It probably sounds a bit trite, but ultimately if you're doing stuff that you're proud of, the rest will take care of itself.

The nights you fail are as important to your development as the nights you do well. They're your battle scars. It's very freeing to experience something that most people are terrified of, and survive it.

Did you ever have a 'eureka' moment in your career when things fell into place? If so, what?
I'm not sure there is such a thing. I remember a comic once told me that stand-up is a ten year apprenticeship, and I'm inclined to agree. I always feel like I'm learning.

What is the best thing about this job?

It's very pure. You can have an idea at 4.00pm, and then do it on stage that night. Within a few hours, you've realized the idea. There's nothing else I've done that moves that fast, and where you have that much control. You are the writer, director and performer. I think that immediacy is what makes it so creatively attractive.

What's the worst thing about this job?

There's no map. You've got to find your own way. And there's very little control. All you can do is work at it hard and get as good as you can, but beyond a certain point, you're relying on other people giving you opportunities.

What would be a typical working day for you?

I try not to get up too late – it's easy with this job to fall into bad sleeping patterns. And I try to spend about four hours writing every day – whether I'm working on a new stand-up show or script stuff or whatever. After hours of writing on my own, my brain and ideas tend to disintegrate.

What makes a good gig?

I think my favourite gigs are where the audience is focused. It's amazing how your performance flourishes when every detail and nuance is being noticed. You find texture to your performance and writing that you didn't even know was there.

What makes a bad gig?

Aggression: I find aggressive audiences and aggressive comedians really toxic.

Any tips on dealing with hecklers?

Just talk to them – give them enough rope and they'll hang themselves. Remember: you're sober and you have the microphone. That's a huge advantage.

What advice would you offer someone starting out in this business?

Work as much as you can. Get out there as many nights a week as possible and learn your craft. And if you're working with someone who you admire, don't be afraid to ask them questions. Most comics love talking about comedy, and it can really open up your approach. I became very good friends with another comic who started at the same time as me, and whenever he worked with someone he admired, he'd ask them for tips before he went on. At first I thought that was a bit weird, but then I realized the wealth of knowledge he was

tapping into, so I started doing the same thing. Talking to the old pros is one of the joys of doing this strange job.

Pat Condell

Pat is a comedian who has been everywhere and done everything. One of the most intelligent political comedians of his generation, his website www.patcondell.net is a popular bookmark for many comedians who look forward to his next bitter, incisive rant.

What do you know now that you wish you'd known at the beginning of your career?
Good jokes come from strong opinions. If you filter the world through your own core values and beliefs, absurdities will abound and the jokes will write themselves.

Did you ever have a 'eureka' moment in your career when things fell into place? If so, what?
Back in the 80s, appearing regularly at the infamous Tunnel Club taught me that a hostile audience is a thing to be laughed at and baited, not feared.

What is the best thing about this job?
You can speak your mind and you have the added pleasure of making it funny.

What's the worst thing about this job?
Travelling on motorways, killing time in strange towns and coming off stage knowing you haven't given your best.

What would be a typical working day for you?
I write every day in a room with no phone or Internet connection. If I'm doing a show in the evening, I'll go over the material and try to improve it. If not, I work on new stuff.

What makes a good gig?
For me, a good gig is where I'm doing my own show with nobody else on the bill. A good circuit gig is one that starts on time; the audience clearly wants to laugh; the compère gets the room focused, then gets off; all your jokes get big laughs; you get paid in full; and nobody comes up to you afterwards to give you 'a joke you can use'.

What makes a bad gig?

Not getting laughs, and if that happens it's not the gig's fault – it's always your fault, and I do mean always. However, there are plenty of things you could use as an excuse: free admission; no lights or PA; the compère staying on too long (any MC who does more than ten minutes at the top of the show and more than three minutes between acts should be pelted with rotten fruit). Other factors might be: noise from the bar; a local 'personality' who likes to sit at the front and heckle; you have to follow someone who's made a mess on the stage, or who has covered the same topics as you; you got there early because you were supposed to open, but now you've been told you have to close; one of the other acts brings a group of friends who laugh uproariously at all their jokes but talk loudly through your set; one of the other acts doesn't turn up at all and you have to do a double set, even though you've got another gig to go to.

But none of these things can turn a gig on their own; the power is always with you to make it good or bad.

Any tips on dealing with hecklers?

Remember why you're there and keep your sense of humour. Witty put-downs are great if you can think of them, but as long as you stay in the funny zone you'll be OK. The worst thing you can do with a heckler is to lose your temper, because if you don't think the situation is funny the audience won't either. At best they'll be laughing at you, not with you, and if that happens you might as well say goodnight. To be honest, I've never met a heckler I didn't want to punch in the face. But I've only ever actually done it once, at a New Variety gig in the 80s, and only because a gang of drunks had wandered in and were ruining it for everyone, particularly for me. I was a lot more impetuous in those days, and before I knew it I had stepped off the stage and given one of them a wallop. I wasn't proud of myself, especially when he went crashing through a door into a room where the gig organizers were counting the box office while sharing a joint. They nearly shat themselves, and as a result I was banned from all their venues for a couple of years.

What advice would you offer someone starting out in this business?

Write every day; never tell a joke you don't believe; respect the audience by always doing your very best; don't steal material, and never take anything personally.

Katy Bagshaw

Katy is probably the newest comic whose opinions were canvassed. She is a young, twenty-something comic who is working at the coalface of the comedy industry. At the time of writing, she is at that weird stage in her career where she is headlining some clubs and completely unknown at others.

What do you know now that you wish you'd known at the beginning of your career?

That this isn't the best way to get over being bullied as a child: therapy is available. And that the audience aren't really that scary.

Did you ever have a 'eureka' moment in your career when things fell into place? If so, what?

Becoming Geordie. I started off with a posh middle class persona and can now be as bigoted as I like.

What is the best thing about this job?

The glory of a gig gone well and the HUGE amount of money I earn (no, really).

What's the worst thing about this job?

The horror of a gig gone wrong. And having to sit and listen to other comedians who go on and on and on about how good they are, especially when they're not. And comedians who write their own reviews (you know who you are).

What would be a typical working day for you?
Get out of bed at midday. Have breakfast. Fall asleep in my eggs. Wake up, check emails. Fall asleep. Wake up in time to get a shower, get out. Be funny. Go back to bed. But then I do have narcolepsy.

What makes a good gig?

A well-run venue: a good mike; good lighting; all of the audience can see the stage; helpful and approachable staff; a decent amount of money (i.e. not 20 pence).

What makes a bad gig?

A badly run gig: background noise; broken mike; no light; pillars obscuring the stage; hen party in the back room; promoter who insults; no money.

Any tips on dealing with hecklers?

Don't try to be funny – say whatever comes into your head and it'll mostly be funny. See them as 'people in a pub' – that's all they are.

What advice would you offer someone starting out in this business?

Stick at it – it takes most people at least two years to crack it. If you don't like the way things are going, feel free to change your set, character, presentation and so on. Keep going until it feels right.

Marek Larwood

Marek is a professional, jobbing comic who has travelled all over the country, winning awards, playing massive venues and performing at late night university gigs. He is endlessly creative and loves to take risks on stage. More recently, he has started to crop up regularly on TV sketch shows and as one third of the comedy group 'We Are Klang' has developed a cult status at festivals around the world.

What do you know now that you wish you'd known at the beginning of your career?

Do what you think is funny and ignore any advice anyone gives you.

Did you ever have a 'eureka' moment in your career when things fell into place? If so, what?

I don't think there is such a thing as a eureka moment. A good stand-up has lots of little eureka moments, when a bit of material falls into place or you think of an ending to a joke. I suppose thinking of a new character or a new way of performing is the closest I've come to a eureka moment.

What is the best thing about this job?

Not being stuck in an office for eight hours a day. It's great being able to think of an idea and then go and perform it on stage that night.

What's the worst thing about this job?

Having a bad gig then going to the toilet and overhearing punters saying '...that last guy was shit'; followed by the awkward moment when they notice your presence; followed by the uncomfortable silence as you wash your hands; followed by the five hour journey home to address the fact there are now 100 more people in this world that think you are a dick. Now I'm so thick skinned I can't even slash my own wrists when it does go wrong.

What would be a typical working day for you?

Every day is different. One day you might be on a train back from Scotland, another day you could be filming something or recording a bit for radio or rehearsing. That all sounds very exciting and positive. You could also be stuck in a ropey bed and breakfast where the heating doesn't work and the bed stinks of someone else's piss or maybe you're at the start of a seven hour car journey with a comic you strongly suspect is a practising sex offender.

What makes a good gig?

There are a lot of things out of the hands of the comic: lighting; sound system; seating; whether the bar is closed; whether you can hear music coming in from the pub next door. It is nice having a gig set up properly where you know what happens is in your hands rather than looking at the room and praying for a miracle.

What makes a bad gig?

Forty pensioners in Portsmouth expecting end of the pier gags.

Any tips on dealing with hecklers?

Most hecklers hang themselves with their own drunkenness. You can always learn stock heckle put-downs, but the best thing to do is to think of something on the spur of the moment. It doesn't even have to be that funny and you get more credit for it. On the rare occasion you are subjected to a genuinely funny heckle, you should give the heckler credit.

What advice would you offer someone starting out in this business?

You can spend all the time in the world you want watching comedy and talking about it. The best way to learn is to go out and actually do it, although I previously said to ignore all advice. I have spoken to a lot of new comics and some make the mistake of thinking this is a stepping-stone to fame and glory. I think to be good you have to love thinking about comedy and writing about it, almost so it is second nature to do it. I think you have to have a love of writing and performing and a self-belief to get anywhere. Also, I must add I went on a course taught by the wonderful author of this book. It gave me the confidence to start stand-up, and I met a lot of people so it wasn't such a lonely journey. Also, it was through the course that I met Steve Hall and Greg Davies who I formed sketch group 'We Are Klang' with.

Since forming we have become almost total pricks.

Mark Maier

Mark has performed all over the world, often topping the bills at the bigger venues. He also is a prolific award winning comedy writer and has had many comedy plays performed on Radio 4.

What do you know now that you wish you'd known at the beginning of your career?
That the less you try, the less forced your material is, the more an audience will give you. If you can 'appear' relaxed, then you are more than half way there. This is a difficult thing to learn and only comes with experience.

Did you ever have a 'eureka' moment in your career when things fell into place? If so, what?
When I compèred a comedy show at the Glastonbury Festival and found that being at ease and not the bag of nerves I was pre-gig was the best thing that could happen.

What is the best thing about this job?
Coming up with a thought that you genuinely don't know is funny until you perform it in front of a group of strangers and hearing laughter.

What's the worst thing about this job?
Any gig in Milton Keynes.

What would be a typical working day for you?
Get up, remind myself where I am working that evening and then spend a couple of hours trying to tailor my material to suit that particular gig. If I'm not working that evening, then... not get up.

What makes a good gig?
An audience who is there primarily to see comedy and appreciate the fact that you are there to make them laugh.

What makes a bad gig?
Disorganization on the part of the venue: bad sound and lighting; no stage; the audience a million miles away from the comedians; or starting a club in Milton Keynes.

Any tips on dealing with hecklers?
Use what they say as opposed to coming up with a standard heckle put-down you have heard before. Chances are, someone else in the audience will have heard the standard line and heckle you for being unoriginal.

What advice would you offer someone starting out in this business?

Be true to yourself and record how your material goes on stage. It took me a couple of years of pretty constant gigging before I felt completely comfortable with myself on stage. There are gigs that go brilliantly and others that are disastrous but you must constantly be working in order to get some consistency to your performances. By recording your material you can hear what has worked as apposed to what you perceive has worked, which is often a very different thing.

Robin Ince

Robin is a force of nature who seems to be responsible (or at least knows the person who is responsible) for all the light entertainment output on television. His name constantly crops up in TV credits. His work ethic and his networking skills are truly frightening. He is also a comedian who delights in taking risks; he recently set up the Book Club, which has been winning praise left, right and centre for helping to reinvigorate the London comedy scene.

What do you know now that you wish you'd known at the beginning of your career?

Why on earth I wanted to stand in front of a group of people showing off in the desperate hope they would laugh. And I still don't know now, it must be something that happened as a child I would imagine: perhaps a beating or getting lost in a big cave. I think the best thing to know at the start is that it doesn't matter where your contemporaries are going and their success, just focus on what you are doing. So many comedians get caught up in getting bitter and that can only get in the way of what you're doing. Also, don't believe what other comedians tell you, they may well be lying. For example, I was told: 'If a joke doesn't work three times, bin it.' Not true, it depends on finding the right audience, the right delivery and so on. Most of the people who tell you this are the comedians you'll find rummaging through your bins at 3.00am.

Did you ever have a 'eureka' moment in your career when things fell into place? If so, what?

My first real eureka moment was doing the So You Think You're Funny competition in Edinburgh. I came second and felt that there must be something in it.

What is the best thing about this job?
You are in control of what you do: even if you fail, you can hopefully fail on your terms. You get to travel the country and possibly the world, showing off and being rewarded for it.

What's the worst thing about this job?
The creeping self-doubt that haunts you, and the way that the odd bad gig hangs in the memory for so much longer than the good gigs. Even a great gig can be marred by the thought of that one line you felt you screwed up.

As you spend so much time on your own, there is plenty of time for lengthy train journeys of self-criticism.

Oh, and never do a vanity search on the Internet, there will always be someone out there who detests you for some reason.

What would be a typical working day for you?
I am something of a whore so days are never that typical. Daytime is either spent writing scripts for others, doing radio shows and all that kind of thing. Then getting panicked because I realize that I've taken too much on and don't reckon I'll get to Skipton on time, and how on earth am I going to get back from there the next morning in time to spout on some BBC7 show? At that point I promise myself that I have learnt my lesson and shall never get in such a tangle again. Then the next month arrives and the tangling starts all over. If you are self-employed, you always presume it's about to end, so fear ever saying 'No'.

What makes a good gig?
A low level of intoxicants in both the audience's and your bloodstream; a microphone that doesn't cut out every time you reach a punchline; chairs that have not been used in any historical inquisitions and not too many people in party hats with poppers and harmonicas.

What makes a bad gig?
All the above in preponderance.

Any tips on dealing with hecklers?
Use a poison dart. If you don't have a poison dart, don't get overly embroiled with them and make sure the audience have heard what they've shouted if you have a specific response to their words.

Sometimes hecklers are actually shouting out nice things or funny thing. If the heckler has been funny, accept that they have been funny rather then just being vicious and swearing at them.

Violent responses to hecklers can look like you are losing grip.

Though there are many clichéd put-downs, it's good if you can deal with them individually. Try not to burst into tears – it may show weakness.

What advice would you offer someone starting out in this business?

Tenacity is the main thing. Your career could go up and down and up, and if you really want to do it you will somehow keep going. There are very few overnight sensations: it might be 10 or 20 years before you get where you hoped, and then when you get there you'll want to be at the next stage, so try and enjoy it as you go along.

Greg Davies

In a relatively short period of time, Greg was winning awards and headlining most of the major comedy venues. He has written for television and is part of the celebrated comedy group 'We Are Klang'.

What do you know now that you wish you'd known at the beginning of your career?

I wish I'd known that hecklers, far from being arbiters of comic ability are in the main drunken middle class men who aren't very popular at work/home. When starting out all comics, no matter how they present themselves in a dressing room, are nervous. A bad gig is nothing more than a bad gig.

Did you ever have a 'eureka' moment in your career when things fell into place? If so, what?

You have mini eureka moments throughout your career I think; it is an endlessly fascinating process and one can never afford to think 'I've cracked it.' That said, the realization that if you are enjoying yourself an audience invariably will, was a turning point; being playful and prepared to let go off your carefully prepared material can be a big part of this.

What is the best thing about this job?

Unpredictability; instant feedback; creative fulfilment; massive trousers.

What's the worst thing about this job?
The feeling that you should always be doing something. If you are not gigging you should be writing. Sometimes it's okay to think about other things.

What would be a typical working day for you?
I find a typical day no longer exists but I do get to sit around the house in my pants more often than I ever dreamt... and I dreamt about it for years*.

What makes a good gig?
• When the room has been set up well by the promoter and, if there is one, the compère.
• When an audience comes to a gig placing comedy higher on their agenda than drinking and/or sleeping with someone.
• When a member of that audience after the gig gets drunk, says 'you were the best tonight' and offers to sleep with you.

What makes a bad gig?
A persistent drunken heckler who is impervious to: wit, humiliation, kindness and/or anger. An audience who haven't paid and weren't really expecting comedy – these people are frequently not even seated near you or facing in your direction.

Any tips on dealing with hecklers?
Engage them, give them enough rope and on very rare occasions doff your cap.

What advice would you offer someone starting out in this business?
Try not to say anything on stage that you do not find funny; be resilient; work hard; be selective about the advice you take; eat vegetables; do not smoke as much as I do and try and find the happy land that exists between self-delusion and self-loathing.

*13

12

business

In this chapter you will learn:
- how to begin your career
- how to market yourself
- professional etiquette.

Probably only half of the day-to-day business of being a comedian is involved with offering the public a funny, innovative act on stage; the other half of your career will involve you managing and exploiting any opportunities that will further your career. This means you will have to develop good business practice very quickly. As a comedian you will have to get used to being a one-man or one-woman band. Ultimately, you are responsible for every aspect of your career: publicity, networking, booking the gigs, keeping an ear out for new opportunities – it all comes down to you.

The most important practice in the business side of comedy – and one which is true for any small business – is to BE POLITE. Be nice. No one wants to deal with selfish, rude people. Even if you were the most obnoxious person in the world, a little bit of enlightened self-interest should dictate that you should try to be nice to your fellow performers and the promoters and bookers of comedy clubs; after all these are the people who you will have to work with.

That being said, let's look at the business side of comedy.

How to get started

The benchmark for a new comic starting out is to make an audience laugh for a mere five minutes. This is called an open spot.

The open spot

Usually, you will be performing before or after a professional comedian who will be doing a 20 minute set. The reasoning behind this is that if you make a complete hash of things, you won't ruin the evening completely. Some clubs put the open spots on right at the beginning of the evening, which is foolish in my opinion, because the audience isn't warmed up properly and the club promoter is taking a terrible risk of starting the evening on a bad note if the open spot struggles.

The half spot

Once you have proved to the club promoter that you are funny, they may eventually ask you back to do a half spot. This could be paid or unpaid depending on how stingy the promoter is. Chances are you will get paid and by rights it should be half as much money as the fee for doing a 20 minute slot. From the half spot, you will eventually build your way up to a full, paid gig.

Open spot venues

There is a subset of gigs that have grown up around London and in some of Britain's other major cities that are called Open Spot Clubs. These are clubs where all the acts are doing an unpaid five minutes performance with the possible exception of the last act, who is more established and will be getting some money. These open spot clubs are a mixed blessing. On the one hand, they give you valuable stage time, but on the other they can occasionally be poorly run. Also, if the audience is packed out, and the club promoter is charging five or six pounds on the door, the comedians can begin to feel a little used if they see the promoter walking home with big wads of cash from the fruits of *their* labour. That said, they are a good place to practise your craft. These sorts of venues can be found in the comedy section of listings magazines in most major cities. They are recognizable as the shows that list nine or ten acts and will usually have the helpful phrase: 'Interested acts call the following number...' Call them up, get a gig and begin your apprenticeship.

It is easy for the new comic to put all their energies into open spot gigs and fail to concentrate on proper venues that lead to a career and (much more importantly at the beginning of your career) getting paid. This is understandable; it can seem a hard business, especially when the more established clubs only take newer comedians by personal recommendation. The only thing you can do is work your way slowly up the food chain, getting your foot through the door and building up your reputation. You might think it a hard, uphill struggle to get noticed, but take heart that comedians and club promoters are very good at spreading the word if they see someone who is new and funny. Comedy is a very small world and news travels fast. But don't let that stop you from being proactive and helping the process along.

Learn to market yourself

One of the best ways to publicize yourself is to get out there and blitz the clubs with really funny material until the promoters sit up and notice. But be selective. Some comedians get so bitten by the comedy bug that they will run around town, occasionally doubling-up at two or even three clubs in one evening. This could end up offering you diminishing returns; after all, it is arguable how much time you will have to process the information at the gigs if you are running yourself ragged seven or eight times a week. Particularly if you are still holding down a day job. So try to concentrate, initially, on the better-run open spot clubs (especially if they are in the habit of paying a closing act. Who knows? One day, you could be that act.). Some established clubs run open spot nights that are designed to encourage new acts to come up through the ranks. A good gig here will often guarantee you a paid ten (or at least an open spot that will lead to a paid ten) on one of their regular club nights. A lot of research and pooling of shared information is required of new comedians at the beginning of their careers, so don't be shy of swapping information with your co-workers. Perhaps, after your initial flurry of performances, once you begin to understand the lie of the land in your particular city or area, you should draw up a plan of where you realistically want to be playing in six months' time then try follow it through.

Publicity

Think about having business cards with your phone number (but not necessarily your address – you don't want stalkers!) and email address. Think about setting up a website with some nice pictures that promoters can use for their publicity and, at the very least, an upcoming gig list. Get someone to video you at a good venue on a night when they have a big crowd and have it made into a DVD showreel. I know of two comedians who landed television jobs by having a good quality tape of their first ever stand-up performance.

Phoning for work

Most of the hard work in this business involves phoning up and asking for a gig. Often you will leave a message on someone's answer phone and not hear back, so after a few days you may find you have to start the whole process all over again. If this is the case, don't start getting cross with the promoter or drop into paranoia freefall imagining that everyone thinks you are terrible. Just keep plugging away *politely*. Look at it from the promoter's point of view. Every day they receive hundreds of messages from hundreds of new acts. Until they know you, or have heard of you, you are just another name in the mix. It's nothing personal, but if they responded to every message, they would have no time to eat or sleep. So keep your messages short, businesslike and polite. There is no point getting an attitude just because someone hasn't returned your call. And the more exasperated you begin to sound on your answer machine message, the less likely they will be to phone you back.

Call promoters at a decent time. Some only like business calls in the morning or (if they have a day job) the early evening. Pool information with the other comics and find out when it's best to call. If you annoy or pester these people outside of their working schedule, they will be less inclined to offer you work. Turn up at their venue and introduce yourself (but only when they are having a quiet moment!) so they can put a face to a name. Better still, get a comedian that you know who is on the bill to introduce you. You never know, an act may not turn up and you may get a chance to take their place.

Look at the open forums on comedy websites. These might tell you about up and coming venues. Or give you tips of how to approach a particular club. But take all information on these public forums with a pinch of salt – it's just one person's opinion. Similarly, while talking about forums, think very carefully before you post anything on these sites. What you say could return to haunt you years later. Be as opinionated as you like on stage, if it is getting laughs, but think twice about this when you are in business mode. It pays to be circumspect.

Etiquette

A good comic will be practically invisible before they step on stage. Turn up to the venue, let the promoter know you have arrived and then try to blend into the background. Here are a few golden rules:

- Don't demand a free drink (it happens...).
- Don't snigger loudly and knowingly at another act having a bad time.
- Don't talk at all while other acts are on stage and don't pester other comedians just before they are about to go on stage.
- If you have brought some friends along for moral support, then remember that any bad behaviour from them will reflect poorly on you. If they are drunk, heckling or causing a commotion and the promoter gets wind that they are with you, then you will not be doing your career any favours.

- Don't have a drink before your set. It won't calm your nerves; it will just slow you down.
- Don't be tempted to have several drinks after your performance, so that you have to be carried out of the venue at the end of the evening. This is your workplace. Promoters need to be able to see that you are dependable, reliable and responsible.

Do your time on stage

If you have been booked for five minutes, don't do ten. If you have been booked for ten, don't do fifteen; even if you are being outrageously funny, all you will be doing is cutting into the allotted time of later comics and making the evening run later and later. Most promoters would rather you did a really funny four and a half minutes than a so-so seven minutes that started well, but stuttered away to a poor finish. Be aware how quickly five or ten minutes flies by. Do your homework and prepare your set. Don't be tempted to cram eight minutes of material into five – you will only look rushed and you will still over-run.

If you have to cut it short because some improvized bits with the audience have eaten into your allotted time, then just cut to a strong closing joke. If you haven't got time for that, then wrap up with a loud and proud variation on: 'Thank you. My name's been (FILL IN THE BLANK)! Thank you and goodnight!' Acknowledge the applause and leave.

One good way of keeping to time on stage is to buy a vibrating watch with a stop watch function and set it to your allotted time just before you start. That way, your wrist will receive a silent reminder of when it's time to wrap up. Very few comedy clubs have a prominent clock to tell the time by, and only the bigger clubs have a discreet red light in the lighting rig to let you know when your time is up. It is your job, and yours alone, to make sure you keep to time.

Building your set

As time goes by, you will continue writing more and more new material. Then there is the worry of trying it out and hoping that it won't mess up your existing set structure. This is less of a problem than it seems as even the stuff that you originally wrote is evolving and growing all the time. This process is called 'bedding down' material. You are letting it grow and are starting to inhabit it more and more. The only problem with fleshing out your material and adding more and more funny asides is that you may find that your tight 10 minute set very rapidly becomes a joke-filled 13 or 14 minutes, so that you are constantly finding that you have to shave bits off your set to fit the time slot you have. With all of this happening, it can be difficult to know where to try out completely new ideas and how to fit them into your existing set structure. One solution is to jam an untested bit between two parts of your set that always go down well. That way if the audience don't get it, you can always hit them with something funny to get them back. Do make sure that you try out newer stuff several times in several different ways before you finally give up on it – perhaps, like your older stuff, it too needs to be 'bedded down'.

Take advantage of the relatively anonymous open spot clubs that exist to try out new material (again, you might think of 'topping' and 'tailing' it with jokes that you know work, so that you are giving the new stuff a fighting chance of a good reaction).

The way you order your subjects is entirely up to you. I would firmly advise that you start your set strongly and make sure you finish it with a bang. Apart from that, there is no hard and fast rule. It's probably a good idea to separate routines that are similar or that rely on similar vocal tricks or rhythms. Always work on the weakest parts of your set and attempt to polish them up. Is there any 'deadwood' phrasing? If so, take it out. Are you being clear enough? Is there a better punchline than the weak one you are currently employing? If so, sharpen it up!

Are you losing the audience on the journey? If so, why? Perhaps it's as simple as missing out one simple bridging thought that would carry them to the same conclusion that you have made.

Compèring

Here's one final suggestion for the particularly brave comedian: become a compère. Taking up the job of resident compère at a particular club is a sure-fire way of allowing you to try out *all* the new material you could ever think of. The trouble with compèring (especially to the same regular crowd) is that it goes through your material at a phenomenal rate. Pretty soon, you will hit a pain barrier where you have run out of scripted stuff and you have to rely purely on charm and your ability to come up with funny afterthoughts. This is when a good stint at compèring a show really starts to pay dividends for the individual comic. As a way of forcing you to generate funny stuff under pressure, it has no equal. As a way of training you up to deal with different audiences and building up your confidence, it remains unsurpassed. Arguably Eddie Izzard, Dominic Holland and Mark Lamaar would not be the outstanding comedians they are today if they had not thrown themselves whole-heartedly into the job of compèring regular comedy venues, week in and week out, for months on end.

Beyond stand-up

There is no greater pleasure than hearing a whole room laugh and know that you are responsible for that. But another pleasure that comes a close second is the feeling of empowerment that this business offers you. Producers and other entertainment industry people think, quite rightly, that if we can entertain a crowd with our own thoughts, that we must be good writers. Also, they may see you work and feel that perhaps you could present a TV or radio show, or act in a sitcom, or do the warm-up for a funky new panel show, or be part of the 'ideas' team for a new youth and music show. The sky is the limit.

You may choose, once you are a little established, to work with some other like-minded comics and form some sort of sketch group. You may take a show up to the Edinburgh Festival and gamble a few thousand pounds investment against the chance of you winning awards and getting some television or radio interest out of your project. Why not? Someone has to get noticed.

This is a business where you can't help but endlessly reinvent yourself; it is an industry that consciously encourages you to play with new concepts and identities.

Look at any night of television and think of all the comedy writing opportunities that present themselves; not just the obvious candidates like sitcoms, but think of *who* writes the funny quips on the autocue for the presenter to read out or all the funny put-downs that are being whispered into the game show host's earpiece. Someone is writing all this stuff, and getting paid. Why shouldn't it be you?

Competitions

Over the past ten years there has been a rash of comedy competitions. Some have become regular fixtures with huge sponsorship, decent prize money and an international reputation; some are little more than marketing exercises by individual comedy clubs trying to drum up some interest (and an audience) during the summer months.

Why should you do a competition?

Someone once said that talent competitions are essentially cruel and unfair, *unless you win*. Certainly, this seems a hard enough business without having the indignity of having your worth judged on a particular five minute performance on one particular night. But if a competition has a good reputation, and if you feel ready for it, then it may shave some time off your career plan should you enter it and find yourself through to the finals. Of course what you have to be able to prove, once you've won, is that you have another funny 15 or 20 minutes ready to back it up with. Undeniably, some comedians have won these competitions far too early in their careers and then have had the torture of trying to please tough university crowds or late night comedy clubs when they haven't had much material beyond a tight, funny five minutes. That is a very deep hole to dig yourself out of.

But for a good strong comic who thinks they are ready, a competition can be a good way for you to race ahead of your peers and receive a well-earned publicity boost early on in your career.

Just ask yourself some basic questions before you enter:

- Has the competition got a good reputation?
- What concrete goals are you hoping to get out of it?
- Have you got a thick enough skin to deal with the paranoia and ego-loss that competitions can engender?
- What is the prize? Is it cash? Is it a string of lucrative gigs? If there isn't a prize, then why are you putting in all this hard work? Are the competition organizers just using you? (One British comedian famously worked his way through all the competition heats, finally gaining first place at the final, only to be told that the prize was an open spot at a prestigious

Australian Comedy Club – *but not the air fare to go with it.* That's a long, expensive journey for five minutes.)

- Who is organising the competition? What are their credentials?
- Do you fit the competition's guidelines? The competition rules, for example, may exclude you from entering if you admit to having too many paid gigs under your belt. (Many foreign comedians have got through to the finals of prestigious competitions by saying that they have only performed 'x' amount of shows in this country, but omitting to point out to having worked professionally for several years in their own country.)

It may sound hopelessly optimistic, but if you are funny then eventually your talent *will* get recognized. A competition may speed up this process, but it is not the massive watershed in your career that you may feel it to be at the time. It is only a means to an end – and that end is to climb a little higher up the comedy career ladder.

Festivals

Every year many comedians in Britain and all over the world move *en masse* to the Scottish capital during the month of August for the Edinburgh Fringe Festival. What began after the Second World War as a small experimental arts festival has grown – especially over the last 25 years – into a huge trade show for the comedy industry. Thousands of pounds can be thrown at an individual show in the hope that a 'buzz' builds up around it and that a TV production company, a commissioning editor or radio producer will realize the show's potential and offer you a big, fat contract. In a festival where the average audience size is four men and a dog, though, there is obviously a lot of scope for disappointment and near-bankruptcy. A good Edinburgh Festival can do the individual performer the power of good. Each year, some maverick show, held together with bits of string and no budget to speak of, will become the people's favourite. But, annoyingly, a show that is just as funny may sink without trace simply because it's on at the wrong venue or the wrong time.

If you want to take the gamble and you think you have a good show then give it a go. But bear in mind these following things:

Everyone in Edinburgh makes money apart from you

Rents quadruple; venues hire out their spaces by the hour, charging more for peak time slots; publicists will insist you hire them, otherwise no one will know your show exists; you must have enough posters and leaflets to cover you for an entire month; you may need to hire people to leaflet for you (the big comedy companies hire a team of about 20 people to leaflet all their shows; even if you have the funniest show in the world, your leaflet will be lost under a pile of their glossy brochures).

Choose a good venue and a good time

Research both these things *very carefully*.

Be aware that to be considered a contender you will have to produce a 55 minute show to fit the hour slot you have booked. That doesn't have to be a solo show; often newer comics will gang together to produce a two, three or even four person show for their first Edinburgh Festival. That way they can all split the costs and expenses.

Check out the Edinburgh Fringe website

It offers lots of invaluable advice for the first timer. Check it out if you are interested.

A good Edinburgh Festival will do wonders for your career. But even a so-so time can expand your circle of contacts, lead to many more working opportunities and generally enhance your working reputation. You may find that you are invited to other comedy festivals all over the world on the back of someone seeing you do a particularly good show at the Fringe Festival.

Other comedy festivals

Other major international festivals include the Montreal Comedy Festival and the Adelaide Comedy Festival. These are usually festivals that comedians are invited to by the organizers once they have reached a certain level. At this point, a comedian's agent will be called and negotiations will begin.

Britain can offer some nice festival experiences outside of Edinburgh, and ones that seem a little less 'closed-shop' than some of the international festivals. Glastonbury Festival has included a dedicated comedy marquee for several years now – if you like music festivals, then it's not a bad working holiday. Reading Festival used to have a comedy tent, but you were always competing with the main stage bands to be heard. Several big towns like Brighton, Leicester and occasionally Newcastle run their own comedy festivals. None as yet have the same kudos as the Edinburgh Festival, and they are all much shorter affairs, but they are all very professionally run and are well thought of by comics.

Agents and managers

An agent is someone who, for a percentage of the work you receive through him or her, will actively seek out work for you.

A manager is someone who will traditionally have a more 'hands on' approach to your career. They may micro-manage every aspect of your professional career. For this service they often (but not always) charge a higher per cent commission for any work that you receive through their offices.

Most comedians would bite their right arm off to have either an agent or a manager. They imagine that this miraculous person will somehow push their career into the stratosphere, or at the very least they will do all the phoning around and booking of gigs. Having an agent or manager seems like the Holy Grail for some comedians. Having one means that we feel someone is fighting in our corner for us. It is heartening to know, despite all the knock backs that we receive in this business, that someone has enough belief in us that they think they can make enough money out of their 15 or 20 per cent commission to live on.

Comedians should always remember that although they may be friends with their agent or manager, theirs is primarily a *professional* relationship. If at any time it is not working out between you, you should both have the freedom to sever your ties.

An agent or manager should help your career in ways that you are unable to. They may agree to look after your work diary and book in all your gigs (although, in most people's experience that is a rarity). They *should* send you out for castings that you would otherwise never have heard of; set up meetings with people who may be able to help you; suggest ways of publicizing yourself or how best to put a showreel together or they may be able to push pet projects of yours forward when you feel you have hit a brick wall.

The most important thing that an agent or manager can do is to negotiate for more money on your behalf. This means that you can avoid arguing with promoters or production companies over your worth. You look after the creative side of things; they look after the financial.

Some comedians think that they can relax completely once they have someone working for them, but this is a mistake. You must be as proactive and driven as you were earlier on in your career – think of the agent/manager as another resource for you to utilize. They will not work by themselves – they need your input to help guide your career.

So be proactive!

The ideal person to look after your interests is someone who is very keen on you, young and hungry for success. They should, ideally, have lots of industry contacts. If an agent or manager has too many acts on their books, or a stable of very well established household names and you, then you might legitimately wonder how much time they can devote to you.

Remember
Nice as it is to have someone to organize things for you, the person best placed to manage your career is probably *you*.

your first gig

In this chapter you will learn:
- how to prepare for your first show
- how to behave on the night
- what to do after the gig.

Don't be scared. This is what all your preparation has been leading up to. You should feel excited that you are taking the first step in your new vocation.

Booking the gig

The hardest part when you begin, arguably, is to pick up the phone and try to convince a complete stranger to offer you a five minute slot at their club. The easiest way to do this is to pick up a local listings magazine and make a list of the comedy clubs that you'd like to play and that you could realistically expect to play (you may *want* to play at the Comedy Store in London – but, initially, you probably aren't quite ready yet!). Do some research and check out which venues you think you'd enjoy playing and *then* phone them up. Some people like to have a marathon session on the phone and book in lots of gigs. This is probably the best strategy; otherwise you will have a very sparse gig diary. It is much better to have your second and third gigs lined up after your first show so that you can keep up the momentum. Some venues book months in advance, some a few weeks, so be prepared to drum your heels for a while once you feel you are ready to unleash yourself on the world.

Once you are booked in, continue doing your research: return to the venue on several different nights and try to get a flavour of what the club is like. What's the crowd usually like? Have they a regular compère? What is his or her style like? Ideally, by the time your gig rolls around, you should be champing at the bit to get on stage.

Three or four days before the gig

Bullet point your set and keep familiarizing yourself with the order of jokes. Make sure that you have something up your sleeve to say just in case you forget what your next joke is. Keep reminding yourself that, although your jokes are very important, the audience will have a much better time if they think *you* are having a good time, so don't become too tunnel-visioned about the experience.

Say your set out loud, at normal volume, when you are alone. Perform in front of a mirror. If you have a very close trusted friend, perform to just that one person. The comedian and writer Sally Holloway is of the belief that if you can communicate your jokes to just one person, you can probably convey these thoughts to an entire room. If you do try out your stuff in front of close friends, then by all means accept any constructive criticism they offer; but do remember that you are the one, ultimately, who is in charge.

Time yourself! If you have been booked for five, aim for about four and a half minutes of material – with laughter that should take it to around five minutes. If you can buy a vibrating wrist watch, then familiarize yourself with it until turning it on seems like second nature to you.

The day before the gig

Run through your stuff. Then relax and do something that's fun. Reward yourself. Decide what you are going to wear. Eat good food. Don't drink heavily the night before – it will slow you down up to 24 hours later. Try not to give in to the rising sense of panic that you are experiencing.

Every comedian has felt exactly as jittery as you do before their first performance, so consider yourself in very good company.

On the day of the gig

Try not to panic. Rest assured that, no matter how much you imagine in your head that the experience will go, it will turn out to be completely different; so try to keep yourself flexible.

If it's a weekend you probably won't want to do anything too taxing or too far from home: you'll be too preoccupied with the evening's show. Eat well, but lightly. Drink plenty of fluids! Try not to eat two hours before the show. If you grab a sandwich half an hour before you go on stage it will slow you down.

If the show occurs during the week then try to bury yourself in work (in other words, keep yourself occupied). Perhaps think about your set during lunch, but don't fret about it too much. You should know it backwards by now, if you have been rehearsing. Keep relaxed and quell any surges of adrenaline by stretching your legs, yawning and so on.

On the evening of the gig

Get to the venue in *very* good time. Introduce yourself to whoever is running the club. Then keep out of their way or offer to help out if they need a hand. Check out the room. Ask for a sound check – politely! Do exactly what you feel you have to get into your performance 'head space': walk around the block for a breath of fresh air or retire to a corner with your own thoughts. Some comedians become very gregarious before a performance, some retreat into themselves. So don't worry about how the others on the bill are treating you. It's nothing personal if they appear rude; it's simply that they are also trying to get their head together. Remind yourself that the only important relationship that you have on this particular evening is with the audience – not with your fellow comedians.

Try *not* to think of your set once the audience starts coming in. Trust that it will all be there when the time comes.

Perhaps you would like to buy a drink to wet your lips when you are on stage. Most comedians would advise against something alcoholic. My own personal preference is water with the tiniest drop of lime cordial in it to make my mouth water if it starts to go dry.

Relax. Warm up, if you need to. Collect your thoughts. Watch the crowd. Try to get a feel for them. Ask the compère how long they are likely to do before they introduce you.

On stage

This is your first gig! Well done, you! As you move towards the stage, remember to smile and enjoy the sensation of just having jumped out of an aeroplane without a parachute.

- Look as if you are in charge and, if it suits your persona, look relaxed.
- Take your time. Keep relaxed. DON'T race through the audience's laughter.
- Talk to the audience, not at them.
- Enjoy everything that happens on stage.
- Finish with one of your best jokes. If appropriate, finish with a nice, big energy. Acknowledge the applause; it's the audience's way of thanking you.

After the gig

Don't retreat to the bar and drink yourself insensible with relief. You are still at work. Notice how much more communicative comedians become after they have performed – this might be a good opportunity to swap notes.

Make sure, either during the interval or after the show, to get some feedback from the club promoter. Ask if they'd like you back. Don't do that terrible, middle class thing of half-apologising for your own performance. You won't do yourself any favours if you had a great time and then say (out of false modesty) 'I thought that could have gone better...' Be nice. Even if the promoter isn't (most are).

Remember to go through your set after the gig. What worked? What didn't go down as well as you expected? Did you improvize any funny lines that could be incorporated into your set?

Try to get some sleep despite the massive high you are feeling. Congratulate yourself. You have just done a very scary thing.

14

the future

'The party always moves on.'

Hakim Bey

Each generation feels that they are re-inventing comedy, when in actual fact, with the aid of hindsight, we can see that they have just been re-discovering it for themselves. Each generation feels they are leading a revolution against the mainstream, and then are slightly surprised when a newer generation comes along and calls *them* complacent and reactionary. So it goes. Back in the early 80s, modern comedy in Britain was born out of alternative comedy: a political comedy that promised to be non-sexist, non-racist and tried to ignore easy stereotypes. The next generation saw this as too worthy or too confining and introduced the concept of 'ironic' sexism or racism. Doubtless, the people who follow them will rebel against irony.

No comedian ever feels that they are part of a movement. They are just one person learning, with each passing gig, how to become a better comic. The comedian is the ultimate outsider, asking their audience to question the absurdity of all the things we do.

But, in one sense, we do all belong to a very small, select gang of people that have, through the centuries, had the guts to stand up before a group of strangers and make them laugh. Sixty million people live in the British Isles, out of which 1000–2000 are (at the time of writing) attempting to carve out a career in comedy; only 500–600 are working with any regularity. That is quite an exclusive club (much more exclusive than the Freemasons or a private members club). And we have an open door policy – anyone can join, provided they can prove that they can make audiences laugh.

Comedy encourages us to continue playing with ideas in a way that most people aren't allowed to. We get to make complete fools of ourselves; we ask the audience to come along with us for the ride; we get to say the things that other people wish they'd said and we often find that they find us damned sexy at the same time!

Stand-up keeps us playing with ideas for our entire working lives.

All creativity comes out of play – so keep playing!

What a vibrant, living art form this is: what other profession would have such a broad church of fellow performers – from hacks to visionaries? What other job would offer such extremes of emotions and achievement, from slinking off stage, humiliated, to raising the roof at a thousand-seat venue?

What a brilliant, dangerous, exhilarating, entertaining way to spend your life.

Countless people have had an absolute blast in this business.

Now it's your turn.

Group games force you to think on your feet and 'up' your performance at the same time. They stop you becoming too cerebral and encourage you to 'let go' and enjoy yourself. If you are lucky enough to be working with a group of other comedians, feel free to try the games listed below.

Some basic guidelines for the following games:

- Try to keep yourself open and responsive to your partner or partners.
- *Listen* to what they are saying so that you can react to them.
- Don't feel you have to force yourself to be funny.
- Rely on your basic human communication skills.
- Don't put yourself in charge if you are working with someone else. React to them rather than try to direct them.
- Try, metaphorically, to say 'yes' to every offer, rather than say 'no'.
- And finally (and not wishing to sound overly pessimistic), it is okay to fail. That's the only way we learn.

Learn to let go!

Some people hate performance games. They feel that they are being foolish for no good reason; some idiot (*me*, if they're in my class) has even told them not to *try* to be funny. That makes them even crosser: 'Why am I doing a comedy workshop that doesn't encourage me to be funny?'

Often people can feel at sea because they are being asked to step outside the usual role that they have given themselves. We pigeonhole ourselves as the responsible homeowner, the concerned citizen, Mr or Ms Sensible, the 'cool' person or whatever persona we think fits us. As the years roll by, we become very comfortable with this mask and feel exposed if we are told to put it away and do something new. Try to remember that the 'mask' isn't you and that you are much more than the labels you give yourself. If you cut away every definition that you have built up around yourself, there would still be an infinite amount of you left. That is the part of you that contains the funny ideas; we are trying to uncover the playful you, not the sensible you.

With that in mind, you may find that some of these performance exercises work better in larger groups: a larger group tends to legitimize the madness; if everyone else is behaving like an idiot, then the individual can be carried along by the rest. There is also a certain anonymity provided by groups: the individual can merge into the mass of others, safe in the knowledge that they don't stand out.

So, if you find yourself working in a smaller group, try to be sensitive to what the other people are doing. It is easy to allow a bit of negativity to open the gates of paranoia. If you think you are being judged, your creativity will shut down. If you do that your social editor will have won.

If you are the sort of person who feels self-conscious during these games, then you can always take heart that, ultimately, *no one cares what you do*. Everyone else is just as worried as you are. You will see other people do really funny things one moment and then fail at something the next. You will probably do it too. But try to remember, in the same way that you don't really care about other people's failures (except to learn by them) and you only really celebrate their successes in the workshop, they feel the same way about you and your successes and failures. If we didn't take a risk and occasionally fall flat on our faces, then we would never learn anything. So, try to be bold and learn to throw yourself into things.

Similarly, if that little social controller in your head asks why *is* everyone running around behaving like fools and you can't convince it that messing around is its own reward, then remind yourself that you are just warming up into the business of comedy. These performance games are just there to limber you up. Have you ever seen the film *The Karate Kid*? At the beginning of the film the young hero desperately wants to learn karate, but all his teacher will let him do is clean the car, to get him used to basic martial art moves. So he spends days, just putting wax on the car and taking wax off the car until the movements are second nature to him.

Well, that is what we are doing in a lot of these performance games. You may not necessarily get many stand-alone jokes out of it (although I'm willing to bet you will make other people in the group laugh a lot) but you will be exercising your comedy muscles.

Warming up

Make sure you have a good yawn and stretch to minimize pulling any muscles. Comedians are notoriously unfit, so don't feel that you are about to tackle an Olympic event. It should go without saying that you should have your hands free, so refrain from lighting up a crafty fag during the performance games. Also, turn off your mobile phone to minimize distractions.

In the same way that you free up your body, try to free up your mind. Forget about any worries you may have had before the games and concentrate on just them. The comedian Martin Beaumont has a wonderful phrase for clearing your head. He calls it 'Etch-a-Sketch Head': just shake all those loose thoughts out and try to present us with a blank canvas. We need you to be 'here and now' when trying out these games, not lost in the past (an angry phone conversation five minutes before) or thinking ahead (will the shops still be open when you're finished?). You have set this time aside to work on your comedy, so enjoy the moment.

Warm up games

Naming everything

Imagine you are God on the first day of creation, naming everything. Point at every object you can see and name it with great authority. Do it with enthusiasm. Most people are a little casual to begin with and have to be encouraged to be a little bit more energized. So try to 'rev' yourself up when doing this.

Then, once you are happy with your energy level, repeat the exercise giving everything the wrong name. Try to have the same degree of authority that you had the first time.

Putting your consciousness in different parts of your body

Walk around the room and try to think where your sense of self exists in your body. Do you feel you live in your head? The ancient Chinese thought that the seat of consciousness rested in the belly; some native American tribes ascribed the attribute of courage to the bowels. Is that any stranger than the common western belief that we exist between our ears? The brain is the most complicated part of the nervous system, but that system extends all through your body. Yet we have all seen people who live entirely in their heads. Their body's movement seems clumsy and ungraceful, like it's an afterthought.

Let's try putting our sense of self in different locations in our bodies.

Walk around the room as if your whole sense of self existed in your forehead. How does that make your body behave? Do you feel more earnest? More deliberate? Slower?

Move your sense of self to the eyes. Does this make you more wide-eyed and innocent? Or suspicious? How do you react to the world (and other people) if your whole sense of self comes from the eyes?

Once you have explored that, move to your nose: feel the air passing in and out of your nostrils; try to become aware of any subtle tangs or scents in the air. How does this nose-person behave? Are they snooty? Inquisitive? How do they behave if the nose is where their sense of self resides?

What about your chin?

Put your whole sense of self in to your chest, then your belly, then your bum. If you are working in a group, make someone the temporary boss and have them shout out other areas of the body: 'Shoulders!' or 'Feet!' or 'The top of your head!' You will probably find your behaviour and movement alters greatly. When it's at the top of your head you may find yourself becoming 'floaty' or dithery; when it's in your belly, you may feel more solid or grounded.

It must be stressed that this is just a warm up. No one is going to ask you to do this for 20 minutes on a comedy stage. We are just playing with notions of physicality. If the game gets you out of your head and into your body a little bit more, then it will have achieved its purpose.

Last name, first name

Someone needs to nominate himself or herself as boss to point and click their fingers at someone so that they know it's their turn.

The first person chosen names someone famous. The next person pointed to has to name another famous person whose first name begins with the same letter that the previous famous person's surname started with. (Single word names are allowed.) So it might be something like:

> Kevin Bacon _ Basil Fawlty _ Felicity Kendal _ Keira Knightly _ Kevin Spacey _ Simon Schama _ Sean Connery _ Clive of India _ Indira Ghandi _ Gerald Ford _ Francis Coppola

There must be no repetitions and no hesitations otherwise you are out of the game.

The last one standing wins.

The comic Martin Beaumont also uses a variation on this game where people have to think laterally about a subject. Again, someone is 'boss' to point at the next victim, but this time the next person has to think of something that incorporates the last word. It will make more sense through demonstration:

Someone might say 'table top' so the next person has to start something using the last word, for example 'top gun'. The next person has to use 'gun', so they might come up with 'gun fire', the next person comes up with 'fire alarm', then 'alarm bells', then 'Bell's Palsy'. Good luck to the next one in that particular game! (I suppose you could say 'palsy victim' at a pinch...) Again, any hesitations or repetitions get you kicked out of the game.

Greeting each other as different people

(A group activity that could be altered to a solo game if you don't mind staring at yourself in a mirror)

Once you are happy enough letting go of your physical inhibitions, make someone temporary boss again and have them shout out descriptions of the type of people you should try to become. Here are a few popular favourites:

- Everyone has to be incredibly hungover and then desperately try to hide the fact from everyone else in the group.

- Everyone has to treat everyone else in the room as if they are a bit insane and they, themselves, are trying to be very understanding.
- Everyone is an undercover police officer trying to buy drugs at a rock festival – unfortunately, they aren't very good at pretending to be 'with it'.
- You know that everyone in the group fancies you and, quite frankly, you have had enough…
- Everyone greets each other as if they were a children's performer.
- Everyone is incredibly patronising towards each other.
- Everyone is incredibly fearful that each person they meet might be the murderer that they 'know' is in the room.
- Everyone thinks that they are the person in charge of the room and suspects that everyone else is getting ideas above their station.
- Everyone in the room is a massive fan of everyone they meet.
- Everyone suffers from very low self-esteem.
- Everyone is the geekiest, nerdiest person in the world attempting to be 'cool'.
- Everyone loathes each other, but because they are at a family gathering, they have to give each other a hug.
- Everyone in the room has a shameful secret that they think everyone they meet is hinting at. That's making them increasingly paranoid.
- Everyone is a physical coward trying to assert themselves to everyone they meet.

I'm sure you could think of lots of other suggestions once you get going. I find this a great way to warm up and wake up a group. Some of the suggestions on the list work on the principle of saying one thing and revealing another. It is almost always funny to watch performers 'unwittingly' reveal things about themselves, like the male comedian who tells you he is a devil with women, but is clearly terrified of any encounter. So remember, even though this game is just a warm up, the comedian can always generate a lot of laughs saying one thing, while revealing another – therefore be ready to jot down any funny lines that appear out of nowhere during this game.

'It wasn't me'

This is a game to turn everyone into very bad, melodramatic actors. Once again, the aim is to make the individual lose some of their social inhibitions. This game can never be played too big or too loud. But remember not to strain your voices.

Everyone gets into a circle. Pretend that every acting agent and theatrical booker is watching and that each of you is determined to make an impression on them. One person begins by shouting out some 'hammy' melodramatic variation of the line: 'It wasn't me... It was them.' They then shift the blame to someone else in the circle who must be even more over the top with their delivery. They may be shocked by the accusation or deny it vehemently, but however they feel they must shift the blame to someone else as soon as possible, with something like: 'It couldn't have been me! It must have been them!!' whilst pointing at someone else.

The rest of the circle, mindful that every casting agent in the room is also watching them, must act their little socks off too; gasping and accusing everyone, voicing outrage and shock in equal measures, like some demented chorus.

You will know if you are doing this game correctly because it will feel like a bad costume drama on steroids.

'It was me and...'

This is the follow up to the previous game. It has exactly the same dynamic and requires everyone in the circle to continue to be very bad actors. This time, however, instead of denying the crime, each individual confesses to the crime (to everyone else's shock or dismay); but they explain that they only did it because someone else threatened them with something horrible if they didn't do it. Having thus successfully shifted the blame from themselves they can join the frenzy of denunciation visited on the new person. Until obviously, they blame someone else.

In this game we are say 'yes, and...', whereas in the previous version we were saying a resounding 'no' ('It wasn't me!'). Each game will be different, but it might go something like this:

> **Person 1:** Yes! I admit it! I did run over his foot. And I'd do it again, I tell you. But the only reason why I ran over his foot in the first place was because she (*pointing at someone across the room*) held a loaded gun to my head!

> (*Gasps and exhortations from the crowd*)

> **Person 2:** Yes! I held a gun against their temple, but I'm not a naturally violent person. I only did it because he

(*shifts blame*) said he would microwave my hamster if I didn't.

(*Grown men fainting; the sound of gnashing of teeth and general overacting*)

Person 3: Big deal! So I wanted to chuck her little verminous rodent in a microwave. So what? And, anyway, I only did it because she (*pointing away*) threatened to beat me with sticks if I didn't.

(*Screams of 'Vile criminal!' and 'Burn the monster' are heard from the crowd*)

Well, I'm sure you get the picture. It is a great game for lifting people out of themselves and getting them to flirt with the idea of using extreme attitudes.

After 10 or 15 'turns' you can always get the next 'criminal' to sit down (still in the circle) so that they can continue to be the chorus, but aren't eligible for being chosen again, until everyone has had a chance to try to worm their way out of these hideous crimes.

The last one standing is obviously guilty and should be treated with extreme caution for the rest of the day.

Creativity games

Innocent or guilty

This is another circle game, like the previous two. Each person has to think of a general question, such as: 'Do they like cheese?'; 'Were they rubbish at sports at school?' or 'Are they a good swimmer?' Don't reveal your question! Each person then has to step into the circle, look everyone in the eye in turn and with as much attitude as they can summon up (as if they were judge and jury), answer the question that they have devised, pronouncing judgement on each person they face. The people who are being judged must take it on the chin.

So the person who is pronouncing judgement might say: 'Yes. Never. No. All the time. Wants to, but can't...', and so on. It can be quite funny, because the rest of us have no idea what the question is and are desperately trying to make a pattern out of the information we are provided with.

One of the strengths of the exercise, apart from playing with attitudes, is that it forces the comedian to take charge. They must make a choice and be definite. The players soon lose our interest if they become wishy-washy.

If you are in the circle, waiting for your turn, watch the relationship between the 'judge' and the 'accused'. Often you will see them reacting to each other's signals. The 'judge' may say, dismissively, 'No. Never!' and the 'accused' might hang their head in shame and silently nod in agreement. The 'judge' then bestows one final look and walks away in disgust. Later we might find that the question was as innocuous as 'Do they like eggs in the morning?' but they have played it up as if it is a life sentence being bestowed. This or indeed *any* playing up is to be encouraged.

Similarly, if it is your turn, try to make eye contact with your next victim and savour the moment. Don't rush through it, eager to be finished. *You* are the one in charge, so take charge. A comedian is paid money to play, not to be timid.

Cold reading

This is another circle game. It is the more advanced sister exercise to the previous game. Don't try it unless you feel that everyone has stopped being timid.

In this game you have to think of a general category that you want to apply to everyone in the group; feel free to make it as specific as you like. Again, you must keep it to yourself. Here is a list of some of the things people have come up with in the past:

- What is their favourite magazine?
- How many people have they slept with?
- What would they have for breakfast?
- What sort of comic book character do they remind you of?
- What is their least favourite activity?
- How will they die?
- What year do you think they should have been born in?
- What was the last kind act this person performed?

Then, as in the previous game, every person takes a turn going into the middle and making up an answer, without ever revealing his or her question. The trick is to be definitive and to show bags of attitude. Relish each moment when you get to pronounce on any given individual. In this game you are pretending to be absolutely sure of your ability to 'read' these people. If you can't pick up anything, leave them for the moment and return to them later. Take your time and don't worry about the clock; say exactly what you want about these people. Do remember that no one cares what you say; they certainly won't be hurt or offended. Everyone knows that it is made up rubbish; they all just want to be entertained. So make sure your little social controller is well and truly turned off when playing this.

One unintended side benefit to this game is that it can, sometimes, reveal what sort of 'vibe' you are giving off. If people are generally indicating through their pronouncements that you seem to be very nice and very middle class, or a bit of a hippy or come across as a bit of a 'geezer', then this is useful information that you can use as a comic – either by playing up to it or subverting it. It is always useful, especially as a newer comic, to have an insight into how others see us.

But the main aim of this game is to get you to make up complete, opinionated observations about other people. Remember, your opinions count to the audience. Even if, as in the case of this game, they are made up on the spur of the moment, with little or no hard evidence to back them up.

As an exercise in cold reading, this is a game that you can play by yourself next time you are sitting in a pub or café. Just give yourself a category and jot down, in your notebook, how each person in the place would respond to your criteria. Try to be discreet. You don't want anyone to think you are staring them out!

Yes/No

(A group activity, although it could be adapted for just two people)

This is another circle game. The person who starts will turn to the person on their left and the two of them will have a whole conversation just using the words 'Yes' or 'No'. It might go like this:

'Yes.'
'Yes?'
'Yes!'
'No...'

'Yes!'
'No...'
'YES!'
'...Yes...'

Or it might be as short as:

'No?'
'Yes!'

As soon as the person who initially responded (i.e. the one on the left) feels the conversation is at a close they turn to the person to their left and initiate a totally new, totally different dialogue.

This is a good game for getting people to turn off the bit of them that wants to take over and take charge, because it encourages you to react. It is also worth doing because it so limits the vocabulary; the people doing it really have to work to communicate their message to each other and to us, the audience.

Watch how many full stories or encounters come out of these scenes when people are limited to only two words. A lot of them will be very satisfying to watch, some will even make you laugh, but almost all of them (unless the players get scared and decide not to listen to each other) will have a beginning, a middle and a conclusion. It is almost as if, when humans turn off their conscious selves and simply react, they can't stop themselves from telling stories. Perhaps the gift of narrative is hard-wired into the brain.

Channel hopping

This is an old improvization game. The group is split in half: one half are the audience, while the other half perform. Someone is elected 'boss' and kneels in front of the group of performers, who have to choose a TV programme to act out. When the 'boss' points and clicks at them they must act out that show to the best of their ability until the finger points and clicks at someone else. The boss's choices should be completely random so that the performers don't know what is going to be next or for how long they will have to speak; all the performers should be ready to go at any time.

Once the performing group have had a fair crack of the whip, they can sit down and the other half of the group get to perform. Feel free to choose films instead of TV if you want.

This is a great exercise for the individual in learning to let go. All they have to do is 'switch on' when they are pointed at and to keep talking and acting until the boss moves on. Often very funny moments can arise out of juxtaposition, but that is just a bonus. The real benefit of this game is that it helps us get used to coming up with ideas out of nothing, it helps us concentrate better and sanctions us to behave foolishly.

Three-headed expert

(You need at least four people to do this one; ideally more, so that someone be the audience)

This is an old improvization game I was taught decades ago. You could use it as a follow-up exercise to the previous game.

Three people sit next to each other in a row and an elected boss kneels in front of them, ready to direct the action by pointing and finger clicking different people.

These three people are going to be one personality with three heads, lecturing their audience (if there is one) as if they are a leading authority in their field. Give them a stupid lecture title, such as 'Why bananas are evil', but don't give them any time to prepare.

Each individual person has to pick up the other person's sentence whenever it is their turn (even if it's mid-word) and still ensure that the lecture makes sense. It forces people to be quick on their feet and also helps them realize that they don't have to hold on to some precious idea that they are desperately trying to crowbar into the lecture. If the next person goes off on a tangent then the three-headed expert has to merrily go down that avenue, even if you had just thought up a great gag to resolve the previous thought. Tough! You aren't in charge. Learn to let go.

Like the previous game, the boss's choices of who to point at next should be completely random. He or she may only let you get a couple of words out, or you may get a couple of sentences – whichever it is, learn to let go of the sentence when the finger clicks on someone else; try not to race to the end of the thought.

Here is an example of a good way of playing this game:

Head 1: Bananas are evil because...
(*click*)
Head 3: ...they are the only fruit...
(*click*)
Head 1: ...made by evil dwarves who live in the land of...
(*click*)
Head 2: ...Milton Keynes. We know they are evil because...
(*click*)
Head 1: ...they live in...
(*click*)
Head 3: ...Milton Keynes.

It is satisfying because we like watching the three picking up on each other's cues and running with their suggestions. These three have also probably made us smile by collectively deciding that Milton Keynes is the home of cosmic evil.

Here is an example of a bad way of playing that same game:

Head 1: Bananas are evil because they...
(*click*)
Head 3: ...evil because they are the only fruit...
(*boss clicks at Head 1, but Head 3 carries on for a moment, unwilling to give up on their idea*)
(*rushed*) ...that is yellow...
Head 1: (*not too sure what the last word is*)
...er...yellow and curved like a...
(*click*)
Head 2: (*thinks it safer to repeat the previous couple of words to give them some 'think' time*)
...Ooh, um, like a big evil...
(*click*)
Head 1: (*trying to save the dialogue by taking control*)
They are evil because they are sent here by aliens...
(*boss clicks at Head 3, but again, Head 1 is reluctant to let go*)
...from Alpha Centauri (*recognizes that he/she has overrun again*) Sorry!
Head 3: Sorry? What was the last word?

The whole illusion has broken down. Our egos and our hesitancy have let us down.

Introducing each other with love

The group are the audience while each person stands before them and introduces the next person with an over whelming sense of love, as if they are their biggest fan. Their adoration must border on the obsessive. The last person in the group introduces the first person, at which point you can begin the next game ('Introducing each other with hate').

This is a good game to highlight what can happen if you are playing with an extreme attitude. It's amazing how often funny ideas come out of nowhere if the comedian is absolutely clear what *specifically* they are supposed to be doing and what *attitude* they should be playing. As with every exercise, you must be bold and take risks. Nothing is to be gained by the performer emotionally freezing and mumbling, 'Here's the next act...' The only outcome to 'bailing' on any exercise is that the rest of us will see how *not* to do it. That isn't a bad lesson to learn, as an observer, but it is a wasted opportunity for the performer.

If the participants can beg, borrow or steal a real microphone and sound system for this game and the next one, then so much the better. The sooner new comedians get used to a mike, the sooner they will be ready to go on stage before a live audience.

Introducing each other with hate

This is exactly the same game as before; but this time you absolutely loathe the person you are introducing. Perhaps they stole your jokes, perhaps they stole your live-in partner, but the plain simple fact is that you hate their guts. Luckily, you think you are a professional enough act not to let this get in the way, so you will try to give them a good introduction, but some of that bile you feel will inevitably bleed through.

Once again, when this works it's funny, because we are watching people say one thing and reveal another.

Feel free to tailor this type of game with other emotions. Perhaps everyone could take a turn experimenting with jealousy, or completely patronising the next act.

Sunday Night at the London Palladium

Find a partner then, as a double act, try to warm up the rest of the group by telling them what a great show they are going to see tonight. It is the group's job to act like a really overeager audience, cheering and whooping enthusiastically throughout. Each person in the couple takes a turn in listing what other great star is in the show while their partner adds a little comment or afterthought to go with it. It could be as simple as, 'I'm really looking forward to seeing them, too…' but it could be as weird as you like. For example:

> MC 1: Later on, live on this stage, we have 70s classic pop group Abba! Yes that's right! They've reformed for one night only!
>
> MC 2: To perform open-heart surgery on members of the audience! We've also got the entire population of Belgium!
>
> MC 1: Eating chocolate…
>
> MC 2: …for world peace! We've also got… (and so on)

The braver you are at taking risks, the more the audience will applaud you.

This is a good game for letting people off the hook. Most of the time you will be responding to something your partner says, so it gives you a bit of a safety net because you feel that there is someone to hide behind.

The double act should aim to keep topping each other's suggestions and list of stars until the 'audience' is apoplectic with joy. Then they can announce the final guest and the next two performers can stand up and have a go.

The rest of the group must make sure that the couple performing aren't 'bottling' it or performing under par. It is their job to keep the double act on track. Although they shouldn't try to take over the exercise, if the couple are being a bit shy to start with, then a little (and I stress *little*) good-natured heckling is allowed. Something in the nature of 'We want more' or 'And what do they do?', perhaps.

Dropping the next one in it

There are two ways to play this game. In both cases, feel free to use a microphone and stand if you possess them. It's not, strictly speaking, essential for the game but it's a good opportunity to practise mike technique.

The first version of this involves everyone introducing the next person and explaining to the audience what a treat they have in store, because the next act is going to do something truly amazing. Then they drop their partner in it by promising the audience that the next act will do something very bizarre. The next act has to honour that promise before they are allowed to introduce the next act (who will also be forced to perform some outlandish feat).

People have been forced to attempt performing the entire cannon of Shakespeare in under a minute because of this game; I have seen grown men attempt to belly dance and seen very bad magic tricks, song and dance numbers or strange impressions performed. So really be prepared to make life difficult for the next person you introduce and then watch them squirm.

The next act must try to perform the stunt or, at a last resort, find a really creative way of getting out of it. It is not acceptable to say: 'Sorry, I've hurt my leg. So here's the next act...'

Remember that this is an exercise in creativity, so we want to see you trying to be creative in fulfilling that particular promise. Please also remember that an audience would much rather see you go down with all guns blazing than see you sheepishly get through the exercise trying to be as well behaved as possible. Eventually you will be paid money to be a fool. Fools are allowed to behave like idiots!

If the group is slightly smaller (three or four people), the participants might enjoy a more intensive version of this game whereby people partner up and take turns in making ridiculous promises to the audience as to what their partner will do. It calls for sharper wits, but a bonus to this game is that you have the opportunity to play with different attitudes more thoroughly. Perhaps one of the double-act begins to hate their partner for what they are making them do, or perhaps one pretends to become more despairing at what they see as the loss of their personal dignity. Whatever happens, the couple can have great fun exploring their extended relationship with each other.

The Lord Mayor's Parade

Split the group into two: one half becomes the audience, the other half select which of them is going to be the commentator (if it's a big group and you want to work on your afterthoughts you could have two commentators). The commentator stands behind the audience, who should sitting in a line, looking ahead of themselves. The commentator is going to pretend to be a television announcer describing the Lord Mayor's Parade for the benefit of the viewers at home. They must be full of gravitas and always sure of themselves.

The rest of the performing team then walk across, one by one, in front of the audience doing something stupid, which the commentator has to address. It's a great game for getting the comedian to come up with ideas out of nowhere. They just have to respond and make sense of everything passing before the audience's eyes: if someone is doing a forward roll in front of the audience, they might say, 'And here comes the Royal Marines Gymnastic display... slightly under strength due to recent funding problems...'; if someone staggers by flapping their arms they might say, 'Now we can see the London Guild of Unpowered Flight trying to take to the air' or they might equally say 'Here comes the Bank of England's lucky albatross, always a crowd favourite...' It is the commentator's job to read some sort of pattern out of the chaos he or she is presented with. The other performers can, if they wish, 'gang up' and appear two or three at a time, if they want to provide more of a spectacle. Feel free to utilize any props (newspapers, chairs, coats) to make yourselves look as stupid as possible. The more stupid you are prepared to become as a performer, the funnier this exercise can be. Many people taking part in the 'parade' find the experience hugely liberating as they try to outdo each other in the ridiculousness stakes. Once the commentator or commentators have had a fair crack at the whip, let the other team have a turn and repeat until everyone has had a go.

Tree and branch – the performance version

The written version of this game appears in Chapter 05.

Each person has to stand up and talk to the others on a given specific topic for one minute. They are given that topic *only* when they stand up, so there can be no preparation time. The game is called 'Tree and branch' because even though their subject is the main topic (the 'tree'), they are allowed to 'branch off' on any tangents.

The speaker is completely in charge even if they are talking apparent nonsense. For the purpose of this exercise they are to treat themselves as a world-class expert on the subject.

Here are some subjects that have proved useful in the past, but please feel free to make up your own:

- Why should Christmas be banned?
- Why is global warming good for you?
- Dogs and cats: the ultimate evil
- How to impress on a first date
- How not to impress on a first date
- The worst vegetable in the world
- Things that bend
- Why should children be seen and not heard?
- The British hedgerow
- Sky diving for fun and profit
- How to upset your mother
- How to prevent fires.

As well as a being a very good game for developing creativity, this can also be used as a presentation exercise. It really puts the performer under the spotlight, so we notice every little tick and jerk they make. Are they making eye contact with their audience or staring fixedly above their heads? If so, then this may not be the best way to engage with their audience. Are they fidgeting or rocking, or are they masking their face or twiddling with their hair in some sort of displacement activity? Then they are probably not looking as if they are having a good time, let alone taking charge of the situation. Remember, if your extraneous movement isn't helping your performance, then it is probably hindering your message. (If it doesn't add, it detracts!) Does the performer favour one side of their body over the other? If this is the case, tell them once they have finished. A new performer may not be aware of how their body can be doing one thing when they are trying to say another (like trying to look important and taking an involuntary step backwards, which looks weak).

Have fun with it. If nothing else, it will show you how little time a minute actually is. Most of the group will be sorry that you have to stop so suddenly and can't entertain them for another minute. Or two.

Home shopping TV

Every person must bring in a stupid object and put it into a pile. Each person takes a turn at pulling a different item out of the pile and tries to sell it to the group as if they were a presenter on a TV shopping channel. Each item is a multi-use item: a coat-hanger doesn't just solve your clothing storage needs, it also doubles as a boomerang with a safety bar; use it as an emergency television aerial; explain how it can make a delightful and fashionable hat. The presenter can be as creative and as stupid as they want. What is the item called? How much does it cost? What luxury materials is it made of? Why is this item a 'must have' product that will make everyone's life complete?

If the presenter's creativity flags, the rest of the group can put up their hands to ask pertinent questions. At the end, have a show of hands to see how many people would want one of those items in their lives.

The party trick competition

Feel free to use a microphone if you have access to one, but it isn't essential.

Everyone thinks of a stupid trick that they want to show off to the rest of the group. It can be as basic as performing a forward roll or making a shadow-puppet, or as complicated and as impressive as performing a card trick correctly. In general, the more stupid and pointless the trick is, the better it will serve this game's purpose. But don't let that suggestion limit you: if you want to show off your light German opera singing skills, then go for it! Each person will perform the party trick with as much stage presence as possible, as if they are presenting something that is really fantastic. If anyone isn't able to think of a stupid party trick, then they become the official judge who will come on stage at the end to announce who came first, second and third and any other honourable mentions.

Each contestant, in turn, must introduce themselves with bags of presence and attitude, perform their party trick once they feel the audience has warmed to them, and then wrap up their mini show and take the applause from the audience before leaving gloriously. In other words, it is not enough to simply perform the party trick: each performer must also muster as much stagecraft as they possibly can, 'topping' and 'tailing' their trick to make it look as if they have a perfect right to be performing before a real audience.

The judge must treat their role seriously, too. When they appear 'on stage' to announce the winners at the end, they must behave as if this is as important as the Olympic games.

One of the side benefits of this game is that it takes comics away from the merely verbal. Who is to say that if the group is entertained by a stupid stunt, a paying audience might not appreciate it too?

Stand-up in Great Britain was in freefall in the 1970s. Working comedians were, with a few honourable exceptions, middle-aged men in frilly shirts and bow ties recycling old jokes, most of which had some very dubious racist, misogynist or homophobic undertones. They would trawl a slowly shrinking variety club circuit, trying to get the audience's attention before the bingo started. It's probably fair to say that the profession was viewed as a little 'lowbrow'. The comic was the man shoved on stage to give the strippers a break, or else they were the performer waggling their eyebrows and shouting out strange catchphrases at the Queen during a Royal Variety Performance. Comedy seemed a little tired and old.

Thirty-five years later, stand-up has become a massive art form in the UK. There are in excess of 90 comedy clubs in and around the capital; many universities and colleges run regular comedy nights; every major city has at least one thriving comedy club; there are at least five major stand-up competitions every year; music festivals now have comedy tents competing with the main stage; there are festivals, tours and agencies devoted entirely to the promotion of comedy; there are even one or two university courses devoted to the medium.

How did this sea change occur?

Probably in the birth of a many-headed, squalling, brat of a beast called 'alternative comedy'. Alternative comedy is often shorthanded by journalists as 'non-racist, non-sexist comedy', which doesn't entirely explain what it was about. Neither is it really fair to call it a movement; it was more a loose collection of individuals who were reacting (all in different ways) to the complacency they saw going on around them. Their ethos still affects the modern scene today.

The immediate years before the birth of alternative comedy had seen a rapid and radical politicization of much of the country's youth: punk rock had passed from subculture to mainstream, introducing a new generation to the aesthetic of anarchy and rebellion; popular youth movements like 'Rock Against Racism' had been formed; CND experienced a huge intake of members as many young people looked for a way out of an insane arms race. Personalized fashion flourished; individualism was in the air. Everything was being questioned: diverse national and international struggles were discussed, people were becoming educated on (or at least familiar with) issues concerning the environment, trade wars, apartheid, multi-national corporate behaviour. It was a good time for dissent.

It seemed that after most of the blandness of the 70s, Britain's youth were becoming more politically aware. They were certainly questioning with greater frequency the traditional values that were shoved upon them. Given their changing opinions, it's not surprising that many young people felt alienated from the 'safe' entertainment marketed on the nation's televisions. How could *Love Thy Neighbour* (a sitcom whose comedy premise was to have a white racist living next door to a black couple) relate to young adults? What did *Terry and June* mean to anyone outside of the suburbs? For anyone who missed this BBC offering, it featured a middle-aged couple worrying 'What will the neighbours think?' endlessly – for decades! It was never off the TV! For anyone with half a brain, popular comedy was a vast desert with nothing to offer in terms of entertainment. Given this, it was only a matter of time before people created their own alternative to it.

It must be stressed at the outset that alternative comedy consisted of only a handful of performers. They were an eclectic bunch with no shared ideology as such. What united them all in the early days was their shared distrust of any authority, whether it was the police, US foreign policy, the judicial system or (a great source of alternative humour) the Conservative government.

The birth of alternative comedy

Alternative comedy began in London in 1979 with two different groups of people.

The first group was a loose collection of performers who opened a venue in the function room of The Elgin pub in Ladbroke Grove. They were all politically minded comedians – feminists, anarchists and plain old die-in-the-wool socialists – who were used to working in political theatre. It was one of their number, Tony Allen, who came up with the title 'Alternative Cabaret'. Although, as he explains, it originally had very different connotations in his mind:

'I was really against Arts Council funding, because I thought the economics should determine the style, and I couldn't understand how you could get these large amounts of money from the Arts Council and then put on something with 30 people in the audience; if you were good and it worked you should fill the place and be able to make a living out of it. So we formed 'Alternative Cabaret' – which is what I called the thing – and we all became 'Alternative Comedians.'[1]

The term soon caught on.

About the same time, Peter Rosengard and Don Ward were opening The Comedy Store in Soho. Rosengard's inspiration came from having had a great night out at the Los Angeles Comedy Store. He thought the concept would work in London. It wasn't the first time that American comedy has influenced its British cousin, but it was, perhaps, the most overt. Rosengard's brazen theft (of even the name!) has, as far as I'm aware, never led to the lawyers being called in.

Rosengard imagined The Comedy Store to be a venue where comedians of any persuasion could play. He didn't really care if they told 'mother-in-law' jokes or denounced capitalism, as long as they were funny. He convinced the owner of the strip club that was to house the event that the Comedy Store was an idea whose time had come. The fact that the owner, Don Ward, was an ex-comedian himself may have made him more sympathetic to Rosengard's idea.

With hindsight, Rosengard would claim that the Comedy Store's aims were clear from the outset: 'Anything went, as long as it wasn't racist or sexist'[2]. This differs from the memories of original performers who were there on the opening night. According to comedian Lee Cornes:

'Rosengard couldn't care less what went on from the beginning. That ethos came from the alternative cabaret mob – Tony Allen, Jim Barclay and Andy de la Tour. My stuff was outrageously racist and sexist at the time but no one mentioned it.'[3]

It was the consequent work of these three people, and a few others, that ousted the sexist and racist comedians from the Comedy Store. Innovative comedy was encouraged; clichéd and stereotypical humour wasn't.

They hired a then unknown but highly abrasive comic called Alexei Sayle for their opening night, who's aggressive style summed up the spirit of the bear pit that the Comedy Store could evoke. Sayle became to some the archetypal Comedy Store comic: loud, scathing and abusive. His style was to influence many alternative comedians who started after him.

There was a third group who helped midwife the birth of the alternative comedy scene, although they appeared slightly later in 1982. They came from an established London theatre company that was trying to move away from the world of 'straight' theatre. They were called 'Cast'.

Cast had been around for a long time; formed by Claire and Roland Muldoon in 1965 as a breakaway from the left wing Unity Theatre. By the 80s, through luck and good management, they found themselves in receipt of Arts Council funding and sponsorship from the GLC. They began to build up a small circuit of venues for their shows. These venues were later well placed to run their successful 'New Variety' nights. From the outset, Cast tried to offer their audience something different. Roland Muldoon explains:

> 'We agreed that what was not needed was five male stand-ups being naughty in Soho à la America, but that the tradition in Britain would go back to variety. This coincided with our need to recruit people who could play out to the audience...with specific interest in promoting entertaining performers as opposed to entertaining comedians.'[4]

In other words, they were interested in pushing the envelope.

The Cast circuit was quite small, with only four or five venues operating at any given time, but they were a welcome addition to the comedians of that time. Despite their very best efforts to nurture radical new variety acts (I saw my first and only 'Marxist Magician' on a Cast/New Variety night), quite a few comedians snuck in through the back door. To them, Cast was a particular boon because they treated you like a professional and (more importantly) *paid* you like a professional. They planted the seed in many comics that what seemed to be an engaging hobby could become a career.

There were many diverse influences, apart from 1970s youth culture, that helped create alternative comedy. Among the most important of these were: the American tradition of stand-up, British music hall, university revue, ranting poets, punk rock, feminism and Thatcherism.

To a greater or lesser effect, they continue to influence modern comedy. Perhaps we should take a brief look at some of the most important ones.

The tradition of American stand-up comedy

The Americans have a long history of stand-up comedy that grew out of the twin traditions of Vaudeville and Burlesque. Whereas British comedy seemed to get stuck in a music hall world, with the emphasis on broad, brash performances, its American counterpart managed to escape these roots and develop into a more intimate style of one man, a microphone and his audience. The advent of the solo stand-up comic occurred in the States around the time of the Second World War. Comedians by the late 50s and early 60s had separated into two groups.

The first were 'gag merchants' or 'one-liner' comics. Their sets consisted of a string of jokes, with little editorial control over content. Material would often be swapped between comedians (or more often stolen from one another). The humour was often generic in style, with little difference between individual performers' styles.

The second group of comedians had a much broader impact on alternative comedy and on modern comedy in general. These comics were more concerned with entertaining through biographical or 'pretend-biographical' information. Broadly speaking, their jokes moved away from the third person ('A man walks into a bar...') to the first person ('A funny thing happened to me on the way to the theatre...'). *Comedy became personal.* This group were responsible for the birth of observational comedy, whereby common experiences or situations were commented on and poked fun at. This type of comedian was far more concerned with social dilemmas and (as they moved into the 60s) with psychological perspectives too. Their routines would take the shape of a voyage of discovery, delighting or outraging their audiences as they progressed. Many of these comics honed their craft in the bohemian atmosphere of the Greenwich Village cafés of New York, although the vast majority took their chances in the more mainstream clubs of the big cities. Hugely influential comedians like Mort Sahl, Bob Newhart and George Carlin began this way, as did Woody Allen and Lenny Bruce. Whereas Allen cornered the market in comedy based on neurosis or psychological disorder (influencing a whole generation of comedians by opening up vast subject areas previously not considered to be funny), it was Lenny Bruce who left a legacy for taboo-breaking jokes that the alternative comics were to adopt a quarter of a century later. This through line continues into modern-day comedy; every few years a firebrand comedian appears to shake us all up.

Bruce died in 1966, after being hounded for years by charges of obscenity. As a role model, he continues to haunt us all. As Tony Allen sometimes says when he ends his set on a rough night:

'Lenny Bruce finished his career out of his head on drugs, hassled by the police and dying in a toilet... That's how I started off!'

Individual examples aside, it's fair to say that Britain adopted the American style of stand-up almost totally during the 60s and 70s. However, by only copying the 'gag merchant' style of the 50s US comedians, with its emphasis on jokes rather than personality, British stand-up effectively painted itself into an arid, uncreative corner that led, almost inevitably, to a reaction against it with the birth of the alternative comedian.

Jokes, by themselves, removed from any context, can only make people laugh. Good comics want to do more than that...

Music hall

Although it was on the wane by the late 50s, music hall still holds a place in the imagination of the British people. Some comedians, from the alternative movement to more modern times, have plundered this heritage in search of comic ideas. Back in the 80s, as we have seen, the Cast/New Variety evenings made a conscious effort to encourage music hall style act. Many of these old styles were spoofed or twisted for audience (hence Ian Saville, the 'Marxist M came across earlier). Sometimes music hall's style might be adopted wholesale, as in the performance of a three-headed ventriloquist and a mind-reading rat called 'Magritte'. Sometimes music hall would be only glancingly referred to; Sean Hughes had a lovely little non sequitur in his set where he would whip out a playing card from his top pocket and ask a bemused member of the audience, 'Is that the card you were thinking of?' before carrying on with his set. Musical acts, magicians, ventriloquists and the outright bizarre often appeared in alternative comedy shows and, by extension, continue to crop up in the world of modern comedy. Al Murray, before he came up with the Pub Landlord character, used to play a very worrying character (who may or may not have been a contract killer) and would entertain audiences by doing impressions of guns and rifles being fired. I would argue that this act owed a debt, ultimately, to music hall.

Steve Murray (no relation) had a marvellously dark act where he would perform standard magician's tricks, such as sawing the lady in two, with teddy bears. What made the act so delightful and so horrible is that the teddy bears were invariably mutilated and would bleed profusely. Here, Steve was subverting the tradition of grandstanding, music hall illusionists.

Dave Schnieder, now perhaps best known as a television writer, used to give the audience a variation on a plate-spinning act; but instead of plates, he would attempt to keep four or five members of the audience spinning on stage.

'The Bastard Son of Tommy Cooper' brought the tradition of sword swallowing to modern comedy audiences.

A good idea is hard to keep down. In more recent times, the female double act 'A Congress of Oddities' have impressed audiences and critics alike with their dark, Victoriana-inspired cabaret.

Aesthetically, there may be a less obvious bridge between music hall and modern comedy that alternative humour tapped into. According to theatre historian Roger Wilmut, music hall originally contained satire and subversion, but as the 20th century rolled on it became a much tamer medium. It seems that when things become too safe or too mainstream then a (usually younger) group come along to kick over the traces.

Comics of the 1980s and 90s picked up on this need for subversion and, under the umbrella of 'alternative', decided to become a voice of dissent.

In the case of music hall, its slow death after the Second World War meant that the world was ready for some fresh voices of protest; which leads us nicely onto the next influence on alternative comedy.

The university revue

One of the functions of humour in society should be to question authority. Satire implicitly poses questions like: 'Is this law right?'; 'Is this a just war?'; 'Are these politicians making the right decision?' By the 1960s few comedians were asking these questions. Music hall had lost its teeth (and was dying out anyway) and television and radio were too staid and 'pro-establishment' to bite the hand that fed them. Britain was coming out of years of rationing and austerity, a new generation was growing up questioning the attitudes of a fading British Empire. Rather like that emergence of alternative comedy, the time was ripe for a new batch of humorists to appear.

They were found in student revues mostly from Oxford and Cambridge Universities. Revue burst onto the scene in 1960 with shows like 'Beyond the Fringe' and their stars went on to dominate television and radio for the next two decades, producing writer/performers such as: Eleanor Bron, Peter Cook, John Cleese, John Bird, John Fortune, Tim Brooke-Taylor, Graham Chapman, Eric Idle, Michael Palin, Jonathan Miller and Alan Bennett.

These comedians often brought a sense of the absurd to their performances and writing that made them rise above the instinct of 'just' poking an accusing finger at society; they tried to treat comedy as liberating play. They were not bound by convention. The best example of this (and one that was to prove a definite influence on alternative comedians and those who came after) is the four series of television's much celebrated *Monty Python's Flying Circus*.

With exceptions like monologists such as Peter Cook or Alan Bennett, most performers were happier working in a sketch format. There was little or no interaction with the audience as there is usually in stand-up, but it was the 'mood' of their work rather than their operation that was to prove a lasting legacy up to the present day.

At best, there is a charming brutality, an erudition and willingness to shatter taboos that most modern co admire and are happy to emulate. The major failings of this 'Oxbridge Mafia' (as they came to be known) were that they failed to democratize comedy in any way. It became the exclusive preserve of a lucky few (mostly white, male and middle-class) who went to the 'right' college and who wrangled a job at the BBC afterwards. They managed to make comedy seem like a closed shop.

As the 60s and 70s rolled by, the rot set in and intelligent comedy became the rarefied domain of a mere handful. Despite the egalitarian mood of the times, there was an unspoken status or (dare we say it?) a class structure to much of it. Comic references to Proust or Kierkergaard's journals may have intended to be satirical, but they implied knowledge that most people working nine to five didn't have time for. The inference in some of these performers' work seemed to be that if you 'got' the references then you were clever enough to join the club.

Ranting poets

Ranting poetry was a high-energy performance style that sprang out of punk rock roots. The self-styled poets would often support bands and have the thankless task of performing before hostile or indifferent audiences. Such a baptism of fire ensured that the successful poets were usually loud, political and funny: a necessary combination of talents if they hoped to get their message across to their listeners.

Performers like John Cooper-Clarke, Attila the Stockbroker, Seething Wells, Ginger Tom, Little Brother, Joolz, Mark Miwurdz and Henry Normal began their careers a year or two before the arrival of alternative comedy. The strange names weren't just there for dramatic effect; often they were used as pseudonyms to help fool the social security system, but as the performers' fame grew, the names stuck with them.

Several poets made the cross over into stand-up, like Mark Miwurdz who, as Mark Hurst, showed his mastery over drunken, late night audiences at the Comedy Store countless of times. Others, like Attila the Stockbroker, have remained poets but occasionally are known to perform at stand-up venues.

Often there remains a blurred line between poet and comedian that performers are more than happy to cross and re-cross. As Henry Normal once put it on stage, 'These are just gags that rhyme.'

It is difficult to say how much ranting poets contributed to the development of modern comedy: they did provide a vital injection of energy in the nascent alternative scene. Perhaps their biggest contribution, back in those early days, was to convince a generation of aspiring comedians that there was a market for solo performers who wanted to tackle dangerous topics. They showed us that it was possible to make money by speaking our minds.

Now, let's have a brief look at the more oblique, social influences of punk, feminism and Thatcherism.

Punk rock was a phenomenon not limited to the world of music. It spawned a number of popular ideologies for young people, ranging from trendy nihilism ('no future') to a very creative anarchy that spread into a number of different areas, bypassing the traditional means of production: a thriving 'street level' fashion industry was founded; venues and clubs were set up; popular art was influenced, as was the communications industry (advertisers started working with 'punk' artists, most famously with the man who designed the Sex Pistols' album covers, Jamie Reid); new writing was explored, and journalistic careers forged in new magazines and fanzines like *The Face* and *Sniffin' Glue*.

There was a feeling at the time that the whole apparatus of popular culture might be taken away from the few big businesses that ran the whole show, and be reclaimed by the audience. Instead of a 'top down' structure, where the public were told to like what they were given, there was more a mood that we could all make up our own minds. Punk encouraged people not to be passive consumers, but to be active participants. If we were all creating our own music, our own literature and our own fashion, perhaps the next logical step (for some) was to create our own humour.

Feminism also contributed to the process of development in modern comedy. Since the early 60s, women were asking why TV and radio comedies were constantly portraying them either as battleaxes or dizzy dolly birds, with few role models to choose from in between. This didn't reflect their experience. They were sick of being treated as objects in the media. Such a constant battle was bound to radicalize the nation's youth, even if it was only a tiny amount. As a generation of women started reorienting themselves, young men found they had to adapt or die. Even the crassest men began to realize that there was no point in offering to give up your seat on the tube if you weren't rewarded with a look of gratitude, but instead got a look of contempt. Female comics found a willing audience who wanted to hear what their individual world-view was. A generation went to war against the lazy stereotypes that existed previously.

This new awareness effectively killed the 'mother-in-law' gag. 'Blonde' jokes were out too (for a while, misogyny tried to creep through the back door with a succession of 'Essex girl' jokes). Any male comic telling jokes whose punchlines revolved around putting down the opposite sex was viewed as old-fashioned and slightly distasteful, like watching re-runs of white folk blacking-up on *The Black and White Minstrel Show*.

Lazy observations about women continue to be made to this day, as do other forms of derogatory humour, but these days it seems to be through the occasional ignorance of young male comics, rather than a default position of comedy as a whole.

Thatcherism is the last influence that I want to look at that played a part in the development of alternative comedy. That particular Conservative government gave us a massive target to aim at.

For a while, it seemed that Ben Elton made a career out of attacking the Conservatives, especially with his weekly alternative address to the nation as the front man for the television show *Saturday Live*.

There was a lot to attack:

Clause 28 was trying to push gay people back into the closet. The 'suss' law gave *carte blanche* to black men being stopped and searched for no good reason. Whole communities were being uprooted through deregulation and sell offs; instead of sympathy and protection, people were told to 'get on your bike' and look for work – any work – even if it meant the break up of the family. The right to strike for fairer conditions seemed under threat. Britain was governed by a regime that supported apartheid in South Africa and shook hands with torturers. Norman Lamont, after wiping billions off the stock market through his own complacency, went on record jokingly saying, '*Je ne regret rien*'. The mood was summed up at a party conference when Margaret Thatcher told us: 'There is no such thing as society.' Sleaze and corruption abounded: brown paper envelopes stuffed with notes were finding their way into the back pockets of MPs; prostitutes were given bribes to keep quiet even though, the public were assured, nothing had happened.

How could any young comedian, angry at the sense of injustice everywhere, *not* comment on these events?

Here, at last, was a really objectionable political party for critical comedians to get their teeth into!

Anger can be a great engine of creativity for the comedian to utilize and it seemed for a while that every week there was something new for comedians to get cross about. But it's difficult to remain angry, over the years, if nothing ever changes. Experience tends to transmute anger into bitter acceptance or cynicism – which isn't the same thing at all.

Over time, the posturing of comedians against the times began to seem a little ritualised. As comedian John Junkin once said, he didn't like it if the audience were cheering rather than laughing; it made the gig seem more like a political rally than a comedy evening.

Some time over the past 15 years, the term 'alternative' was quietly dropped: perhaps it seemed a little old fashioned. Modern comedy in Britain stopped being a reaction against the mainstream in a few rooms above pubs or in back rooms and *became* the new mainstream. Comedy is now seen as a legitimate career choice in a way that wouldn't have been possible 20 years ago.

The pioneering spirit of alternative comedy fled long ago; perhaps its demise was inevitable, given the constant turnover in fashions and fads. Perhaps every artistic movement can only last a brief time before burning itself out or becoming swamped by the mainstream culture it began in criticizing. This seems to have been the fate of alternative comedy. Comedians began by lampooning daytime TV gameshows and now we host them; we were bored by primetime sitcoms and now we write them. In a very real sense, comics of a certain age have become the new old guard.

Let's not be too pessimistic. As stated, comedy is also a thriving international scene, due in no small measure to what British comedians tried to achieve in the 1980s. There are more clubs, more festivals, more comedy TV and radio being produced than ever before, and this shows no sign of abating.

This is one of the lasting legacies of alternative comedy: it created a network of venues around the country where audiences can see comedy and where performers can work out their apprenticeship. This training ground is invaluable; it is where you will be honing your craft throughout your career.

The second lasting legacy of alternative comedy was to make overt sexism and racism unpopular, discouraging inaccurate stereotypes. Perhaps it helped force comics to not rely on what they thought an audience would want them to say, but instead encouraged them to speak their own minds. Out with the 'Englishman, Irishman and Scotsman' jokes; in with the personal observations.

The rot always manages to creep back in, however. We may not tell jokes deriding black people, Jews, women or the handicapped anymore, but we will all (with no sense of the social injustice of it all) continue to lampoon the Welsh, Americans, fat people or the old. What makes the first group forbidden and the second fair game for the comedian? Have the goalposts actually moved that much? Or did we just substitute one set of stereotypes for another?

Also, despite all the non-racist, non-sexist talk at its inception, modern comedy continues to be the province of mostly white, middle-class men. Likely as not, this just reflects the makeup of society. Ben Elton observes:

> 'People say to me, "Why aren't more women doing it?" Well, why aren't there more women doctors? It's because we live in a sexist society. It doesn't help to lie about it.' [5]

This is perhaps a debate for another day, perhaps for another generation of comics. Let's leave the final word about alternative comedy to Tony Allen:

> 'It shifted the mainstream a little bit – but to move the mainstream just a little bit you have to get out there and go HEAVE!! And I think that's what we did.'[6]

NOTES

[1] [4] [5] and [6] Wilmut, R. & Rosengard , P. *Didn't You Kill My Mother in Law?* London, Methuen, 1989

[2] and [3] From an article by J. Conner in the now defunct listings magazine *City Limits* entitled 'Game for a Laugh', 1989

taking it further

Further reading

Allen, T. (2002) *Attitude*, Glastonbury: Gothic Image.

Banks, M. and Swift, A. (1987) *The Joke's On Us*, London: Pandora.

Angerford, L. and Lea, A. (1979) *Thundersqueak*, TMTS.

Berger, P. (1985) *The Last Laugh*, New York: First Limelight.

Freud, S. (1994 edn.) *Jokes and their Relation to the Unconscious*, London: Penguin.

Jacobi, S. (2005) *Laughing Matters*, London: Century.

Koestler, A. (1964) *The Act of Creation*, London: Hutchinson & Co.

Orwell, G. (2004 edn.) *Why I Write*, London: Penguin.

Philotunus, A. (2002) *The Good, the Bad, the Funny*, The Mouse that Spins.

For more information about Logan Murray's comedy courses, contact him at email@loganmurray.com or look at his website www.loganmurray.com.

index

From Advanced Sudoku to Zulu, you'll find everything you need in the **teach yourself** range, in books, on CD and on DVD.

Visit **www.teachyourself.co.uk** for more details.

Advanced Sudoku and Kakuro
Afrikaans
Alexander Technique
Algebra
Ancient Greek
Applied Psychology
Arabic
Aromatherapy
Art History
Astrology
Astronomy
AutoCAD 2004
AutoCAD 2007
Ayurveda
Baby Massage and Yoga
Baby Signing
Baby Sleep
Bach Flower Remedies
Backgammon
Ballroom Dancing
Basic Accounting
Basic Computer Skills
Basic Mathematics
Beauty
Beekeeping
Beginner's Arabic Script
Beginner's Chinese Script
Beginner's Dutch

Beginner's French
Beginner's German
Beginner's Greek
Beginner's Greek Script
Beginner's Hindi
Beginner's Italian
Beginner's Japanese
Beginner's Japanese Script
Beginner's Latin
Beginner's Mandarin Chinese
Beginner's Portuguese
Beginner's Russian
Beginner's Russian Script
Beginner's Spanish
Beginner's Turkish
Beginner's Urdu Script
Bengali
Better Bridge
Better Chess
Better Driving
Better Handwriting
Biblical Hebrew
Biology
Birdwatching
Blogging
Body Language
Book Keeping
Brazilian Portuguese

Bridge
British Empire, The
British Monarchy from Henry
  VIII, The
Buddhism
Bulgarian
Business Chinese
Business French
Business Japanese
Business Plans
Business Spanish
Business Studies
Buying a Home in France
Buying a Home in Italy
Buying a Home in Portugal
Buying a Home in Spain
C++
Calculus
Calligraphy
Cantonese
Car Buying and Maintenance
Card Games
Catalan
Chess
Chi Kung
Chinese Medicine
Christianity
Classical Music
Coaching
Cold War, The
Collecting
Computing for the Over 50s
Consulting
Copywriting
Correct English
Counselling
Creative Writing
Cricket
Croatian
Crystal Healing
CVs
Czech
Danish
Decluttering
Desktop Publishing
Detox

Digital Home Movie Making
Digital Photography
Dog Training
Drawing
Dream Interpretation
Dutch
Dutch Conversation
Dutch Dictionary
Dutch Grammar
Eastern Philosophy
Electronics
English as a Foreign Language
English for International
  Business
English Grammar
English Grammar as a Foreign
  Language
English Vocabulary
Entrepreneurship
Estonian
Ethics
Excel 2003
Feng Shui
Film Making
Film Studies
Finance for Non-Financial
  Managers
Finnish
First World War, The
Fitness
Flash 8
Flash MX
Flexible Working
Flirting
Flower Arranging
Franchising
French
French Conversation
French Dictionary
French Grammar
French Phrasebook
French Starter Kit
French Verbs
French Vocabulary
Freud
Gaelic

Gardening
Genetics
Geology
German
German Conversation
German Grammar
German Phrasebook
German Verbs
German Vocabulary
Globalization
Go
Golf
Good Study Skills
Great Sex
Greek
Greek Conversation
Greek Phrasebook
Growing Your Business
Guitar
Gulf Arabic
Hand Reflexology
Hausa
Herbal Medicine
Hieroglyphics
Hindi
Hindi Conversation
Hinduism
History of Ireland, The
Home PC Maintenance and
  Networking
How to DJ
How to Run a Marathon
How to Win at Casino Games
How to Win at Horse Racing
How to Win at Online Gambling
How to Win at Poker
How to Write a Blockbuster
Human Anatomy & Physiology
Hungarian
Icelandic
Improve Your French
Improve Your German
Improve Your Italian
Improve Your Spanish
Improving Your Employability

Indian Head Massage
Indonesian
Instant French
Instant German
Instant Greek
Instant Italian
Instant Japanese
Instant Portuguese
Instant Russian
Instant Spanish
Internet, The
Irish
Irish Conversation
Irish Grammar
Islam
Italian
Italian Conversation
Italian Grammar
Italian Phrasebook
Italian Starter Kit
Italian Verbs
Italian Vocabulary
Japanese
Japanese Conversation
Java
JavaScript
Jazz
Jewellery Making
Judaism
Jung
Kama Sutra, The
Keeping Aquarium Fish
Keeping Pigs
Keeping Poultry
Keeping a Rabbit
Knitting
Korean
Latin
Latin American Spanish
Latin Dictionary
Latin Grammar
Latvian
Letter Writing Skills
Life at 50: For Men
Life at 50: For Women

Life Coaching
Linguistics
LINUX
Lithuanian
Magic
Mahjong
Malay
Managing Stress
Managing Your Own Career
Mandarin Chinese
Mandarin Chinese Conversation
Marketing
Marx
Massage
Mathematics
Meditation
Middle East Since 1945, The
Modern China
Modern Hebrew
Modern Persian
Mosaics
Music Theory
Mussolini's Italy
Nazi Germany
Negotiating
Nepali
New Testament Greek
NLP
Norwegian
Norwegian Conversation
Old English
One-Day French
One-Day French – the DVD
One-Day German
One-Day Greek
One-Day Italian
One-Day Portuguese
One-Day Spanish
One-Day Spanish – the DVD
Origami
Owning a Cat
Owning a Horse
Panjabi
PC Networking for Small
  Businesses

Personal Safety and Self
  Defence
Philosophy
Philosophy of Mind
Philosophy of Religion
Photography
Photoshop
PHP with MySQL
Physics
Piano
Pilates
Planning Your Wedding
Polish
Polish Conversation
Politics
Portuguese
Portuguese Conversation
Portuguese Grammar
Portuguese Phrasebook
Postmodernism
Pottery
PowerPoint 2003
PR
Project Management
Psychology
Quick Fix French Grammar
Quick Fix German Grammar
Quick Fix Italian Grammar
Quick Fix Spanish Grammar
Quick Fix: Access 2002
Quick Fix: Excel 2000
Quick Fix: Excel 2002
Quick Fix: HTML
Quick Fix: Windows XP
Quick Fix: Word
Quilting
Recruitment
Reflexology
Reiki
Relaxation
Retaining Staff
Romanian
Running Your Own Business
Russian
Russian Conversation

Russian Grammar
Sage Line 50
Sanskrit
Screenwriting
Second World War, The
Serbian
Setting Up a Small Business
Shorthand Pitman 2000
Sikhism
Singing
Slovene
Small Business Accounting
Small Business Health Check
Songwriting
Spanish
Spanish Conversation
Spanish Dictionary
Spanish Grammar
Spanish Phrasebook
Spanish Starter Kit
Spanish Verbs
Spanish Vocabulary
Speaking On Special Occasions
Speed Reading
Stalin's Russia
Stand Up Comedy
Statistics
Stop Smoking
Sudoku
Swahili
Swahili Dictionary
Swedish
Swedish Conversation
Tagalog
Tai Chi
Tantric Sex
Tap Dancing
Teaching English as a Foreign
   Language
Teams & Team Working
Thai
Theatre
Time Management
Tracing Your Family History
Training

Travel Writing
Trigonometry
Turkish
Turkish Conversation
Twentieth Century USA
Typing
Ukrainian
Understanding Tax for Small
   Businesses
Understanding Terrorism
Urdu
Vietnamese
Visual Basic
Volcanoes
Watercolour Painting
Weight Control through Diet &
   Exercise
Welsh
Welsh Dictionary
Welsh Grammar
Wills & Probate
Windows XP
Wine Tasting
Winning at Job Interviews
Word 2003
World Cultures: China
World Cultures: England
World Cultures: Germany
World Cultures: Italy
World Cultures: Japan
World Cultures: Portugal
World Cultures: Russia
World Cultures: Spain
World Cultures: Wales
World Faiths
Writing Crime Fiction
Writing for Children
Writing for Magazines
Writing a Novel
Writing Poetry
Xhosa
Yiddish
Yoga
Zen
Zulu

teach
yourself

speaking on special occasions
roger mason

- Are you worried about making a speech?
- Do you want to know where to begin and what to cover?
- Would you like examples of what works?

Speaking on Special Occasions explains how to plan and
make a good speech, whatever the occasion. It will give you
strategies for dealing with nerves and building your confidence,
so that both you and your audience enjoy your speech.

Roger Mason is an experienced speaker and writer.

| teach yourself | **songwriting** |
| | sam inglis |

- Do you want to write songs, but don't know where to start?
- Would you like practical advice on creating music and lyrics?
- Do you want an insider's guide to how modern music is made?

Songwriting shows you how to write great songs even if you've got no musical training. It explains how to come up with ideas, how to build 'hooks' into finished songs, and how to use a PC as a songwriting tool. An audio CD takes you through writing a song step by step, and there's essential information on recording, promoting and performing your music.

Sam Inglis is Features Editor of 'Sound On Sound', the world's leading music recording magazine.

teach yourself

theatre
nicholas gibbs

- Are you interested in acting, producing, or directing?
- Do you want to find the right theatre group?
- Would you like to gain confidence and skills?

Theatre offers a wealth of guidance for everyone interested in drama, whether as an actor, producer or lighting technician. It covers everything from finding a local theatre group to recruiting professional experts, raising funds and staging a show, and features lots of useful contacts and essential resources.

Nicholas Gibbs is a writer and director/producer who has worked on a wide variety of theatrical and radio productions.

teach
yourself

writing a play
lesley bown & ann gawthorpe

- Do you need creative guidance?
- Do you want to learn the basics of dialogue?
- Would you like advice on staging and related areas?

Writing a Play covers both the creative and practical elements, with plenty of interactive exercises and examples. Covering everything from character development to stagecraft, it explains how to write for both amateur and professional theatre, with plenty of advice for taking it further.

Lesley Bown and **Ann Gawthorpe** are prize-winning writers. They have been working and writing together for over ten years, producing over 13 plays for amateur and professional theatre groups, and broadcast productions.